Sisters
and Quilts
Threads That Bind

Ann Seely and Joyce Stewart

Threads That Bind

The threads that bind us heart to heart
And keep us near though far apart,
Are threads that last throughout the years
Of sisterhood and joy and tears.

Our quilts are records of the past,
The seams are stitched with care to last.
To comfort, brighten, warm and cheer
The hearts of friends and family dear.

They're filled with memories, joy and pain,
Woven to cherish, they'll ever remain
As symbols of our sisterhood,
And love that's binding, strong and good.

Shari Jo Shirley

POSSIBILITIES®

8970 East Hampden Ave., Denver, Colorado 80231
303-740-6206   FAX 303-220-7424

Dedication

This book is dedicated to our parents, Allen M. and Ava Winterton.
Our dad quietly supports us, and our mom brags about us to everyone she sees!

Special thanks to our husbands, Richard D. Seely and Lynn J. Stewart.
And to our children and grandchildren:
Michael, David, and Steven Seely
Ron and Susan Watkins - Trevor, Tyson, Shari, and Staci
Greg and Lisa Stewart - Brandon
Jim and Shari Jo Shirley - Scot
Steven Stewart
Allen Stewart

Credits

Photography–Brian Birlauf
Illustrator– Marilyn Robinson
Electronic Illustrator–Lynn Pike
Graphic Design–Marilyn Robinson, Sharon Holmes
Editor–Sharon Holmes

Table of Contents

Sisters' Profile

Joyce and Ann were born in American Fork, Utah and raised in Orem, Utah. Both attended Brigham Young University. Joyce currently lives with her family in Rexburg, Idaho, and Ann and her family live in Salt Lake City, Utah. Joyce began quilting in 1981 when asked to piece a quilt for her church group. Not long after that, when she discovered that she could make quilts faster by strip piecing methods, and that she could buy books exclusively on quilting, and that there were quilt groups she could join, she was hooked! In 1982 she introduced Ann to quilting, and they have been enjoying it together ever since. Both have taught quilting classes in area quilt shops, have won numerous awards for their work, and have had their work published in books, magazines, and calendars.

A SAMPLING OF JOYCE'S AWARDS AND PUBLISHED WORK:

Festival of the American West; *Fantasy*; Best of Show; 1984.

Quiltmakers 1987, calendar by Leone Publications; *Another Dimension*; 1987.

American Quilter's Society Show; *Mountain Memories; How Beautiful Upon the Mountains*; 2nd place, Amateur Wall Quilts; 1989.

Great American Quilt Contest III, Discover America; Museum of American Folk Art; Best Interpretation of Theme in the Traditional Style; 1991.

American Quilter's Society Show; *Nihon No Onna No Ko*; 2nd place, Amateur Pieced Quilts; 1991.

American Quilter Magazine; Optic Glow; 1987.

Old-Fashioned Patchwork; Grandmother's Flower Garden; 1989.

Quilt Art Engagement Calendar, American Quilter's Society; *Celebration*; 1991.

Sampler Quilt Calendar, Oxmoor House; *Crossing Over Time*; 1991.

Quilts: The Permanent Collection, American Quilter's Society; *Splendor of the Rajahs*; 1991.

Great American Quilts, Oxmoor House; *Wicker Baskets*; 1992.

A SAMPLING OF ANN'S AWARDS AND PUBLISHED WORK:

Salt Palace Home and Garden Show; People's Choice; 1985.

Great American Quilt Contest III, Discover America; Museum of American Folk Art; Semi-finalist; 1991.

Festival of the American West; Judges' Merit Award; 1991.

High Points Masters Division, Utah Quilt Guild Annual Show; 1991.

Quilter's Newsletter Magazine; Quilts and Other Comforters; 1987.

Quilter's Newsletter Magazine; Big 200 Quilt Contest; *Star of the Earth*; 1988.

Living With Quilts, Meredith Press; *Country Cradle* and *Santa Fe Ottoman*; 1991.

Introduction

Sisters and quilts...what a delightful and enduring combination! We sisters are bound together by our birth, and we are bound together as soulmates by sharing our love of quilts. Each quilt in this book is presented with a photograph of real sisters representing a different phase in the rhythm of life. From childhood through adolescence and into adulthood, our sisters and our quilts provide us with some of our most prized memories. Secrets and confidences are often shared when sleeping under the same quilt as children. The creation of a sister's trousseau quilt provides time for reflecting on the blessings of sisterhood. When a new baby comes along, a sister will often be the first to make a special quilt for the new arrival.

Whether we are sisters by birth or simply sisters in spirit, quilts can bind us together. Follow us now as sisters of all ages share quilts that bespeak the joys of sisterhood. A newly decorated room needs a new quilt. A daughter or niece going off to college must have a new quilt to remind her of home. There are quilts for celebration, quilts for birthdays, and special quilts for dear loved ones who need a little extra love and attention.

Sisters and Quilts: Threads That Bind is a keepsake, a book that shares with its readers different events in the lives of sisters and quilters. We celebrate sisterhood and quilts!

Threads That Bind

The quilt was obviously very old. Many of the silk fabrics had almost disintegrated with time, but still it was beautiful. It was a variation of a Log Cabin, a small square in one corner with logs on only two of the sides. Yes, the fabrics were worn and fading, but it had evidently been well cared for over the years.

The quilt teacher held the quilt up for all to see. "This is a type of Log Cabin quilt quite popular in the mid-1800s. This particular one must have been made by someone who had access to many fabrics because of the variety used in the quilt. I don't have any history of the origin or the maker," she said, "and after I bought it, I noticed it had originally been larger. Someone has cut it in half." Everyone in the class moaned. Who could have possibly ever cut into such an exquisite quilt?

A wagon train was headed west; it was 1852......
Katherine reflected on the events of the past three years as she pulled the quilt up around herself and her sister Lucy. Today had been a happy day; Katherine and Lucy had celebrated their common birthday. Katherine had just turned thirteen and Lucy three. Katherine had been exactly ten years old when her sister was born. How happy she had been to finally have a little sister! All her friends had very large families, and Katherine had wanted a brother or sister for a long time. Finally her wish had come true; she had a sister, a sister born on her own birthday. The family members were all so happy. It seemed as if nothing could ever go wrong. Tragedy struck, however, when Lucy was a year and a half old. Their mother died. Soon after that, Father decided that the little family should move west. Everything was sold, given away or packed into a wagon, and they headed out. In spite of her joy over the birthday celebration earlier in the day, Katherine shivered and pulled the precious quilt closer around them. The quilt was all she had to remind her of her mother and home.

Lucy broke into Katherine's reverie: "Tell me a story," she begged. "Tell me a story from the quilt."

Katherine smiled. Every night was the same. Lucy loved the stories from the quilt, and Katherine loved telling them. It helped her remember happier days.

"Which one?" she asked.

Lucy moved her hand over the quilt until she came to a soft blue patch with flowers on it. "This one, Katy," she said, looking up at her sister. Somehow Lucy found the soft blue patch quite often. It was her favorite story.

"Well," Katherine began, "this one is from a party dress that belonged to a girl with beautiful red hair. Her name was Nell, and everyone said that she was the prettiest girl in town..."

Before long, Lucy was asleep, but Katherine kept looking at the quilt. Each piece is special, she thought, and she began to tell herself some of the stories held within the patches of the quilt. Memories of home, friends, family, and happier times came flowing over her. Mother had been a dressmaker, so nearly every piece was different. Many were fancy silks and brocades from party dresses of the girls in town. Some were from dresses that had belonged to Katherine. One came from baby Lucy's christening gown. One was from a special dress Katherine wore when she was eight. Here a bit of a wedding dress, there a piece from Grandma's apron. This comforting quilt was now the only possession that gave joy and continuity to Katherine's life, and she fell asleep, grateful for its presence in her life and consoled by the comfort it afforded her.

The days moved slowly on, and the little company rolled across the open plains. It was not easy, but they all tried to be as cheerful as possible and to dream of the new and better life ahead. Each night there were the stories from the quilt.

They had been traveling for about three weeks when Lucy fell ill with a fever. Katherine did everything she could to help

Lucy feel better. In the day she would sit with Lucy in the wagon as it lumbered along. She would stroke Lucy's hair, smooth her pillow, and sing. At night she would tell the quilt stories and hold Lucy as she fell asleep to the sound of the chirping crickets. Katherine's heart was wrenched with fear for her precious little sister. She would draw the quilt tightly around them both, and the tears would flow as she sought solace in the quilt's comforting warmth.

One day, late in the afternoon, when they had camped for the day, Katherine left Lucy resting and went to get cool water from a small nearby stream. As she picked up the bucket, a feeling of calm came over her, and she felt that Lucy would be all right very soon.

Katherine walked slowly through the soft grass toward the water. At the stream, she filled her bucket and sat down. The sound of the water was soothing and refreshing as it bubbled over the rocks. Katherine lay back, looked up at the blue sky, and remembered a few comforting words: "This is the day the Lord hath made. Rejoice and be glad in it." Maybe everything will be all right, she thought.

Some time passed, and Katherine told herself she had better get back. She rose, picked up the heavy bucket, and began her way back to the wagon. As she crested the little knoll and looked toward the wagons, she froze. Three men were digging not far from her wagon. "A grave! Lucy!" she screamed. "Lucy! Lucy! Lucy!" Katherine dropped the heavy bucket and began to run. Tears were streaming down her cheeks, and she felt as if her heart would pound right out of her chest as she finally reached the wagon and climbed in.

She began to shake uncontrollably. The quilt was neatly folded in the place that had been Lucy's bed. Katherine stumbled backward, almost falling out of the wagon. In a daze, she made her way to where her father was sitting near the men. He was holding the now still body in his arms. His red, swollen eyes looked up at Katherine, and he said simply, "She's at peace now."

Katherine could only nod her head. She turned, numb with grief, and one of the ladies put an arm around her to lead her back to the wagon. "I'm so sorry, Katherine," the older woman said. "We will need something to wrap her in. It doesn't need to be too big."

Katherine nodded as she climbed into the wagon. Somehow she found her scissors. She carefully picked up the quilt, and with a heavy heart, she began to cut it in half.

by Ann Seely

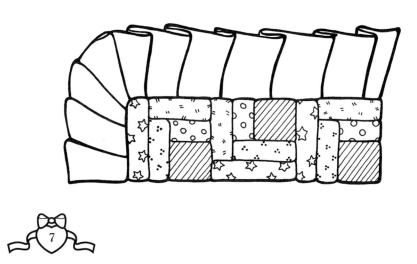

Tools & Equipment

We recommend using the best equipment you can afford. This includes good quality, sharp scissors used only for cutting fabric. Tools such as rotary cutters, cutting mats, and rulers should only be used for the purpose that they are intended. Using the rotary cutter to cut materials other than fabric, or using it without the protective cutting mat will dull the blade. If a blade becomes dull or nicked, change it at once. Keep the rotary cutter out of the reach of children. The special care you give all your quilting aids will ensure that they will provide lasting service.

Adequate lighting is essential for accurate work. If you try to work in a poorly lit area, you are more apt to make mistakes. Two sources of light on opposite sides of your work area will help to eliminate shadowing.

Keep your sewing machine well oiled following the manufacturer's directions. To keep machine free from lint, use a "canned air" product sold at most fabric shops and camera shops; never blow into the machine as the moisture from your breath can cause rust on metal parts. A cover is recommended when the machine is not in use.

BATTING - Use only top quality, brand-name quilt batting. Avoid the temptation to purchase off-brand quilt batting. A poor quality quilt batting will not only be more difficult to quilt but will never give you the beautiful results that come with good quality batting. Thinner bats are easier to hand quilt.

BIAS BARS - Available in a variety of sizes, these thin metal bars are used to make uniform bias tape for applique. They are most helpful for making stems and vines, and are very useful for other narrow applique work such as Celtic applique and stained glass applique.

FABRIC - We strongly recommend using only 100% cotton fabric. It is easy to work with–it responds to steam to aid in easing small excesses, and it presses crisply even when you only finger-press. Your quilt may last for many generations, so you will not want to use inferior fabrics just to save a few pennies now. Using blends in the same quilt with 100% cotton fabrics is not advisable. All fabrics wear differently as we now know from studying antique quilts where many combinations of fabrics were used. We also recommend prewashing fabrics to remove any excess fabric finish, help set colors, and diminish shrinkage problems later.

FRAY CHECK™ - Fray Check™ is a liquid "glue" that when applied to the raw edge of fabric prevents the edge from fraying. It dries clear and is washable. It is useful for applique projects where fraying might be a problem.

LIGHT BOX - This helpful piece of equipment is a box with a transparent top and a light source inside; it can be used to trace patterns from one medium to another, such as from paper quilting patterns onto a quilt top.

NEEDLES - Three types of needles will be needed: a sewing machine needle, a hand sewing needle for applique, and a quilting needle. Always use a sharp sewing machine needle. Do not sew over pins! Change the sewing machine needle often and use a size appropriate to the type of fabric and the size of the thread being used. The ball-point needle for sewing knits will not work well with the cotton fabric used to make quilt tops. An easy way to keep track of sewing machine needles is to use a "tomato" pin cushion and label it with a permanent pen as to the type and size of needle that is kept in each section. For hand sewing and applique work, use sharps;

betweens are used for hand quilting. The larger the number of the needle, the smaller the needle. When hand quilting, you will be able to make smaller stitches if you learn to use a smaller size needle. Number 10 needles are a good choice.

ROTARY TOOLS - A rotary cutter is a razor sharp wheel similar to a pizza cutter. The wheel rolls across fabric, cutting a thin, precise line. A rotary mat is used to protect the surface beneath the fabric. The cutting mat has a self-healing surface and comes in various sizes and colors. Mats may or may not be printed with gridlines. For general cutting, choose a serviceable size, one that will accommodate fabric folded 22″ wide. Smaller mats are portable and very useful for classes. A heavy duty plastic ruler is used to guide the cutter and to measure the cuts. These rulers come in many shapes and sizes. Rotary tools are especially useful for cutting pieces when measurements are given instead of templates and for making border and binding cuts. The use of rotary tools aids the quiltmaker in making cuts more quickly and with greater accuracy.

THREAD - Often not much thought goes into choosing the proper thread until you have had a bad experience with the wrong choice. Just as with fabric and batting, good quality thread will give the desired results. Because many different colors of fabric may be used, it is almost impossible to use a thread that matches everything. A good rule of thumb is to choose a thread that is as dark or darker than your darkest fabric. For hand quilting, use a stronger thread. A thread made specifically for quilting is a natural choice, but often the color choice is limited. A good quality 100% cotton thread is widely available in an excellent range of colors and can be substituted for quilting thread.

WALKING FOOT - This sewing machine attachment is also called an "even-feed" foot. It ensures that layers of fabric will be evenly fed through the sewing machine. Different sewing machine companies have their own version of this foot, and there are generic even-feed feet available also. It is very helpful for sewing binding to the quilt and for some types of machine quilting.

Other needed equipment includes plastic or stiff paper for making templates; iron and ironing board; straight pins; and safety pins for basting the quilt for machine quilting.

There are also many "doo-dads" and specialty items coming on the market every day. Many of these are wonderful, time-saving inventions, and some are just fun to try. As you become more and more interested in quiltmaking, you may want to invest in many of these new tools. You may even invest something yourself!

Glossary of Terms

APPLIQUE - Applique comes from a word that means "applied". This refers to fabric that is applied to another fabric by stitching either by hand or machine. Applique is a decorative feature.

BACKING - This is the fabric that is on the back of the quilt "sandwich". The backing is part of the quilt, so it should be a good quality fabric that relates to the design of the quilt top. Backing can be a solid color or a printed piece. Backing should be prepared two or three inches larger than the top for insurance against shifting.

BATTING - This is the filler that is inside the quilt "sandwich". Batting is discussed in the *Tools and Equipment* section on page 8.

BASTING - Basting refers to the action of assembling the quilt prior to quilting. Basting can be done with large basting needles and fine basting thread or with rustproof safety pins. If basting is done with pins, however, they must be removed as soon as possible. Pin-basting is not recommended in humid areas of the country as rust spots can be caused by the pins. Basting is removed after the quilt is quilted.

BINDING - Binding is the outer edge of the quilt that finishes the raw edges. The binding should be considered an outer border when designing the quilt. The binding takes the most wear in quilts that are used daily and should be made of a double thickness of fabric. Methods of binding are discussed in the *General Directions* section.

CROSSHATCH QUILTING - Parallel quilting lines any distance apart are intersected by parallel quilting lines crossing in another direction. These lines can be quilted vertically and horizontally or on the diagonal, and they can form squares or diamonds depending on the angles of the parallel lines. They are most often used as background quilting to fill large areas.

CUTTING LINE - The outer edge of each patchwork pattern piece in this book is the cutting line. Cutting with precision is as important as stitching with precision.

DIAGONAL SETS - Pieced or appliqued blocks are set on point so that the rows of blocks run diagonally through the quilt.

GRAIN - This is the direction of fibers in fabric. Straight grain can be lengthwise or crosswise. Lengthwise grain runs parallel to the selvage edge and has no stretch. The crosswise grain runs across the fabric from selvage to selvage and has some stretch. Bias is 45° from straight grain and has the greatest amount of stretch. Attention must be given to the direction of the grain when cutting out pieces for blocks. Avoid putting the bias edge on the outside edges of a block whenever possible. In diagonal sets, the large setting triangles around the edge of the quilt center should be cut with the long edge on the straight grain.

HAND PIECING - This is a method of sewing pieces together by hand. It differs from machine piecing in the way the pieces are marked and cut out. See Hand Piecing in the *General Directions* section.

MACHINE PIECING - This is the method of stitching a pieced block together using a sewing machine. The presser foot of the sewing machine is used as a guide to make the ¼" seam. See the *General Directions* section for a more detailed description of machine piecing.

MITERED BORDER - This refers to a border or borders on a quilt where the corner is resolved in a diagonal seam. A method of achieving an easy mitered border is discussed in the *General Directions* section.

QUILTMAKER - More than just someone who makes quilts, a quiltmaker loves geometric shapes, the soft curves of floral applique, the interplay of color, freshly pressed fabric, and the feel of quilting stitches. Quiltmaker is a term of endearment!

SASHING AND SETTING SQUARES - Sashing, sometimes called lattice, refers to strips of fabric used to separate pieced or applique blocks. Setting squares are small squares placed at the intersections of the sashing strips.

SEAM ALLOWANCE - The seam allowance is the distance from the seamline to the cut edge. Quilt piecing generally calls for a ¼″ seam allowance or is trimmed to a ¼″ seam allowance. All pattern pieces in this book use ¼″ seam allowances. Seam allowances in applique are usually slightly less than ¼″.

TEMPLATE - Template is another term for pattern piece. Templates can be made of lightweight plastic (if they are to be used repeatedly) or mid-weight cardboard such as a manila folder. Label templates with a permanent pen and mark the grainline.

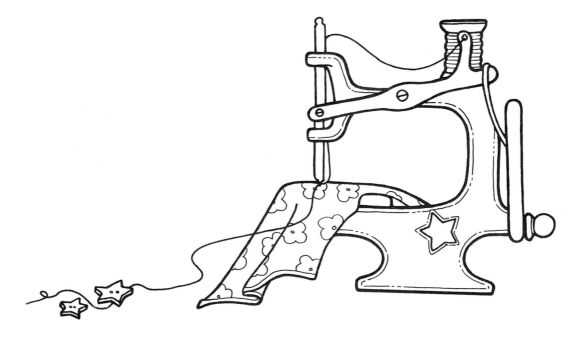

General Directions

FABRIC PREPARATION - We recommend using good quality 100% cotton fabric. Prewash fabric to remove excess dye and to help reduce shrinkage. Separate dark and light fabrics and machine wash in warm water and mild detergent. Clipping the corners with a diagonal cut will cut down on fraying and tangling in the washer. Quarter and eighth yard pieces can be soaked in the sink in warm water and rinsed until the water runs clear. Partially dry fabrics in the dryer and press with a steam iron. It is a good idea to prewash fabrics soon after purchasing them so they will be ready to use.

BEFORE YOU BEGIN - Read through the directions for the chosen pattern to become acquainted with the process. Assemble all the equipment and make sure everything is in good working order. Organizing work space will save precious minutes and prevent frustration. Although some of the quilts appear complex, don't be afraid to attempt any project. If each step is followed carefully and precisely, even a beginner can achieve excellent results. If there are any techniques you need help with, read through the appropriate part of the *General Directions* section.

FINISHING STEPS FOR ALL QUILTS:

1. Press quilt top well.
2. Mark for quilting, if desired.

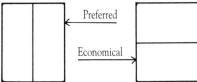

3. If necessary (depending on size), piece backing. Some backings requiring piecing are pieced horizontally to save fabric.

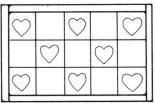

Preferred

Economical

4. Piece batting, if necessary.

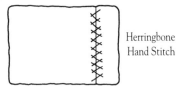

Herringbone
Hand Stitch

5. Layer backing, batting, and quilt top; baste.

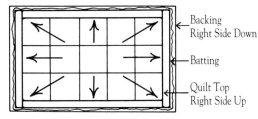

Backing
Right Side Down

Batting

Quilt Top
Right Side Up

6. Quilt by hand or machine, or tie.

7. Bind quilt.

MACHINE PIECING - Method #1 - Using the outer line of each patchwork pattern piece, carefully make templates by tracing onto plastic. Mark each template with a permanent pen and cut out. Trace around the template on the wrong side of the fabric. (Ar in a cutting chart refers to A reversed, a piece that is a mirror image to A, so flip the A template *over* to get Ar.) Line up template on one of the previously marked lines each time it is moved for marking a new piece. Cut apart on marked lines with sharp scissors or a rotary cutter. Accurate cutting allows for more accurate piecing. It is a good idea to cut and sew one block to make sure that everything is correct. Then go ahead and mark all the pieces and cut them out. Sew the pieces according to the pattern guide using an accurate ¼" seam. Check the distance from the needle to the edge of the presser foot to make sure it is ¼". If not, a piece of tape placed ¼" away from the needle can be used as a guide. Press seams to one side, preferably toward the darker fabric whenever possible. Chain stitching saves time; simply feed sets of patches through the machine without cutting the threads between them. Pinning is not usually required on small pieces, but if pins are used, remove them before sewing over them. To sew set-in pieces, sew only to the ¼" seamline and take one stitch back and forth to hold the thread. To set in the next piece, begin stitching at the inside corner and stitch to the outside edge. Repeat for the other seam. Press. After the block is finished, measure it to make sure it is exactly right. Always use the same sewing machine to make all the blocks in a project because even slight differences in sewing will affect the final size of a block.

MACHINE PIECING - METHOD #2 - Make templates, mark, and cut out pattern pieces following the directions for hand piecing. Pin two pieces together, carefully matching the drawn lines. Unless there is a piece to be set in later, sew all the way across the piece from edge to edge. If there is a piece to be set in, the drawn line indicates exactly where to stop sewing and make a small backstitch. After sewing carefully, trim the seam allowance to ¼" and press to the darker fabric.

HAND PIECING - Many quilters prefer to piece by hand. It makes an easy take-along project for waiting times at dentists' offices and children's ball practices. Make templates using the inside line which is the stitching line. Trace around this line on the wrong side of the fabric leaving ½" between pieces for the seam allowance. (Ar in a cutting chart refers to A reversed, a piece that is a mirror image to A, so flip the A template over to get Ar.) Cut out each patch ¼" from drawn line. Stitching is done with a sharp needle and a single thread using a small running stitch. Begin and end stitching on the drawn line; do not stitch into the seam allowance. A small backstitch at the beginning and end of the seam will be sufficient to secure the stitching. When crossing a seam, do not sew the seam allowances down; put the needle through the base of the seam allowances, leaving them free. Press the same as for machine piecing. Periodically check the accuracy of your work.

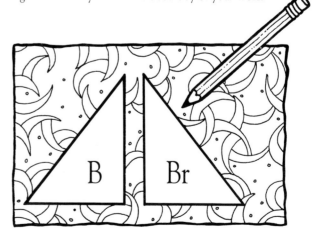

HAND APPLIQUE - Make templates by tracing individual pattern pieces; cut them out on the line. Draw around each template on the right side of the fabric. (Ar in a cutting chart refers to A reversed, a piece that is a mirror image to A, so flip the A template *over* to get Ar.) Cut out a scant ¼″ from the drawn line. Carefully turn the seam allowance to the wrong side and baste in place. Keep the knot on the right side of the fabric so the basting thread can be easily removed later. Position the piece and pin or baste it down. Applique is worked in layers from background to foreground. Using a fine, sharp needle, and thread to match the applique piece, stitch it in place. Applique stitches should be small and totally invisible. Come up from the back (knot is on the underside) and catch one or two threads of the applique piece. Working toward you, stitch around the piece. Inside curves will need to be clipped to allow turning. The underside of the applique should look like a tiny, close running stitch. If pressing is needed, try pressing only the background, taking care not to press lines into the appliques. Generally the fabric behind larger applique pieces is trimmed carefully away. This makes quilting easier, and the applique puffs out nicely.

Cut Out   Clip

To make narrow stems, use a helpful device called a *bias bar*. First, determine the width of the finished stem. Cut bias strips of fabric twice the finished stem width plus ½″ for seam allowance and ease. Bias strips can be seamed together for long vines. Fold the strip in half lengthwise, wrong sides together, and stitch using a *scant ¼″* seam. Insert the flat metal bias bar and press, keeping the seam allowance underneath. Continue to slide the bar along the inside of the strip, pressing as you go.

Slip the bar out when finished pressing. Trim seam, if necessary, so seam allowance will be hidden as stem is appliqued in place. Raw ends should be covered with flowers, leaves, or other applique pieces.

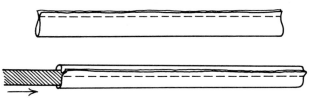

BORDERS - In order to make sure the borders will fit your quilt, measure your top before cutting. Measure the length of the quilt top from edge to edge (across the center, not along one edge) and prepare two borders this length. Sew these borders to the quilt. Then measure the width of the quilt top from edge to edge (again across the center) and prepare two borders this width. If more borders are desired, repeat this process.

MITERED BORDERS - A mitered border gives a somewhat more elegant look to a quilt, and it is not difficult to do. If there are two or more borders, it is easiest to sew them together into one unit first and then treat them as one.

1. Sew two border units that are 3″ to 4″ longer than the sides of the quilt will be when it is finished and two border units that are 3″ to 4″ longer than the top and bottom of the quilt will be when it is finished.

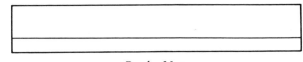

Border Unit

2. For side borders, begin by measuring the length of the quilt across the center. Cut one end of one side border at a 45° angle, making sure the part of the border unit that will go next to the quilt is in the correct position. Measure along the shorter edge of the border unit to a point that corresponds to the length of the quilt. Mark. Cut another 45° angle on this end of the border unit in the opposite direction from the one cut on the other end. Matching ¼″ seam intersections at corners of quilt and on short side of border unit, stitch side border to quilt. Repeat for other side border.

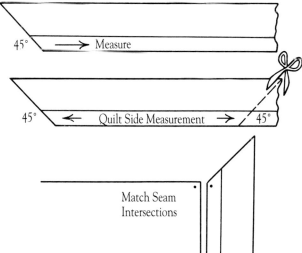

3. Repeat for top and bottom borders.
4. Pin and stitch all four mitered corners; begin at outside edge of quilt and stitch toward seam intersection at inside corner of miter.

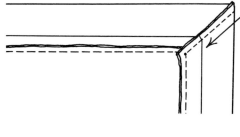

MARKING - Whenever possible, it is best to mark the quilt patterns onto the top before it is assembled with the backing and batting. A light box or a well lighted window can be used when tracing patterns onto the top of a quilt. Tape the pattern to the light box or window so it won't move around, carefully position the top over the pattern, and trace the design. There are many marking pencils available for marking designs. Experiment with them so you know which one suits you best and how it reacts before using it on your quilt.

ASSEMBLING THE QUILT "SANDWICH"

Backing - The backing of the quilt should be washed and pressed. If there are seams in the backing, press them open to cut down on bulk if hand quilting. The backing should be two or three inches larger than the top. One way to ensure a pucker-free back when basting is to tape the backing right side down to a clean floor, keeping it fairly taut.

Batting - Lay the quilt batting on top of the backing and smooth out any wrinkles. Allowing the batting to "rest" for several hours or overnight helps get rid of excessive wrinkles.

Quilt Top - Smooth the quilt top over the backing and batting. Check to make sure the backing and batting extend beyond the top all the way around. Pin the corners and edges of the top and batting to the backing, making sure the quilt top is smooth. Baste the layers together. Baste with a large needle and fine thread and work from the center out. Basting may also be done with rustproof safety pins. Place pins about three or four inches apart. See related information in basting section of *Glossary of Terms*, page 10.

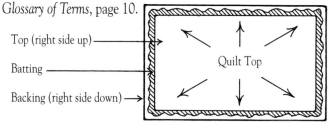

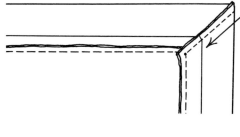

QUILTING - Quilting is the small, even running stitch that holds the quilt sandwich together and gives it a lovely, textured surface. To begin quilting, make a small knot in an 18″ to 20″ single strand of thread. About 1″ from where you want the quilting to begin, go through the top into the batting but do not catch the backing. Pull the knot through, and it will catch in the batting. With a rocking motion, take three or four small running stitches onto the needle and pull the thread through. Continue in this manner, keeping the stitches small and even; stop when the thread is about 5″ to 6″ inches long. To end a line of quilting, make a small, loose knot in the thread and pull it down to the surface of the quilt with the tip of the needle. Take one more stitch into the quilt top and batting, bringing the needle up about one inch away. Clip the thread. Quilting can be done in a small hoop held on your lap or in a large frame. Try several different methods until you find the most comfortable one. For the smallest, most even stitches, use as small a needle as possible and also get used to using a thimble. Remove the basting pins or thread as the quilting stitches are added.

BINDING - The binding is the finishing touch to a quilt. The most desirable binding is double thickness for longer wear. A mitered corner gives a very nice finished look to any quilt.

1. Prepare binding long enough to fit around entire quilt plus extra for turning corners and ending off, about 15 extra inches. Cut binding 2½″ wide on the straight grain. Stitch pieces together with right-angle seams and press seams open. Trim edges of quilt even and baste to prevent shifting.

2. Fold binding in half lengthwise, wrong sides together. Stitch raw edges together with ¼″ seam, using an even-feed foot.

3. Leaving a "tail" about 8″ long, and using a ⅜″ seam allowance, begin to sew binding along one of the side edges of the quilt not too close to the corner. Sew binding through all thicknesses of the quilt. End stitching ⅜″ away from the edge at the corner. Lift presser foot and pull quilt away from machine slightly without cutting threads. Fold binding back to form a 45° angle at the corner and finger-press. Raw edges of quilt and binding should be even.

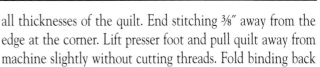

4. Fold the binding down, raw edges even with the next raw edge of the quilt; the folded binding should be even with first raw edge of quilt. Continue stitching from the spot where you stopped in step 3. Repeat miter at each corner.

5. End stitching about 12″ from where it began. Take the quilt away from the machine and work on a flat surface. Lay the loose binding "tails" one over the other on the edge of the quilt and mark the point for seaming them together so they will fit nicely on the quilt without pulling or puckering. Open the binding and stitch the ends right sides together. Test the fit before trimming ends. Trim; press seam open. Refold the binding and finish sewing it to the quilt.

Mark For Seam

Finish Stitching

6. Turn binding to wrong side of quilt and handstitch in place using an invisible stitch and thread to match the binding.

7. Fold the miter on the back of the quilt in the opposite direction to the way it is folded on the front to distribute the bulk. If necessary, stitch the miters closed with an invisible stitch.

The Quilts

Part of the joy of having a sister is the sharing. Through the years sisters share many things: dresses and dolls, bedrooms and bicycles, songs and secrets, prom gowns and poetry. Now we would like to share our love of quiltmaking with you. Each of the fifteen quilts gathered here has a special place in the lives of sisters. Along with each quilt is a picture of real sisters. Some are our friends, and some are our family, but because we believe all quiltmakers are sisters, they are your friends and family, too.

The first quilt, **Victorian Silks**, is based on an actual pioneer quilt we were shown while attending a workshop in northern Utah. This quilt inspired the story, *Threads That Bind* found on page 6. We have a pioneer heritage that includes several families who walked the entire distance from Missouri to Utah in the mid-1800s. We have included this beautiful pioneer quilt and story to honor them. It is shown made of scraps of pure silk, but it would be equally lovely in a variety of calicoes.

The baby quilt, **Buttons and Bows** is designed with a baby girl in mind. The pastel colors are light and airy. A row of delicate pink pieced ribbon blocks adds the perfect touch. An entire nursery could be planned around this entrancing quilt.

Bright Colors is a small quilt that might remind you of the hours you spent coloring or maybe the bright clothes as you played dress-up with your dolls. The many colors seem to twinkle and sparkle right before your eyes.

The sunbonnet girl in our **Roses For Sue** is sure to charm her way into any little girl's heart. Sue has been gathering flowers in her basket, and she holds a rosebud in her hand.

Three sisters share their love for their country with the three teddy bears in the **Teddy Bears on Parade** wallhanging. Marching bears waving flags seem to say, "We love the red, white, and blue!"

Pinwheels and Posies is a twin-sized quilt made in very feminine floral fabric. If sisters are sharing a room, make two!

We cannot forget the teen-ager on your list. **Sweet Sixteen** is a dramatic wall quilt of hot pink hearts entwined with aqua ribbons, a perfect gift for a sixteenth birthday!

For young ladies with a love of music, we have designed **Duet**. It would be beautiful as a bedspread, or maybe it could be tucked away in a hope chest waiting for the "special day".

Speaking of special days, **Friendship Basket** is perfect for signing at the bridal shower. Each guest may choose the basket she likes best to sign and add a bit of advice for the bride-to-be.

The beautiful wallhanging **Bride's Bouquet** will contribute to wedding day memories. Write the names of the bride and groom and their wedding date in the applique heart.

A new home certainly deserves a new quilt. Our **Home Is Where You Hang Your Heart** is a happy reminder of the meaning of home and family.

Another quilt that would be a wonderful addition to any room in your home is **Nighttime Magic**. The deep blue color of the backgound sets off the border of applique flowers, creating the feel of an enchanted forest.

There comes a time in sisters' lives when they are footloose and **Fancy Free**. Bits of fabric gathered from many places become a reminder of those happy times shared with others.

Patchwork and applique combine in the comforting lap quilt, **Calico Charm**. Although it looks complex, it is simple to create. It is a great size for taking the chill off cool evenings.

Our final quilt is the sampler, **Memories**. Twelve blocks are set on point surrounded by an applique border of vines, leaves, and flowers. Your memory quilt will be loved and cherished for many generations to come.

We hope you will enjoy using this book as much as we, as sisters, have enjoyed getting it ready for you. Our wish, now that we have shared our quilts with you, is that you will want to share them with your own special sister. Creating a quilt is making a memory that will last forever.

Victorian Silks

APPROXIMATE SIZE: 54″ x 54″
BLOCK SIZE: 6″ - 64 blocks set 8 x 8
SETTING: Blocks set straight
TECHNIQUES: Strip piecing on a foundation, embroidery, ruffled edging

YARDAGE (42″- 45″ or 107-114 cm wide):

Muslin (foundations)	2⅝ yds. (2.4 m)
Brown velveteen (B)	⅝ yd. (.6 m)
Silk scraps (C, D, E)	to total 2⅝ yds. (2.4 m)
Ruffle	1⅞ yds. (1.8 m)
Backing	3 yds. (2.8 m)
Yellow perle cotton #8	approx. 300 yds. (275 m)

CUTTING (Templates on page 78):

Muslin (foundations)	Template A: 256
Velveteen	Template B: 256
Silk	Template C: 256
	Template D: 512
	Template E: 256
Ruffle	7 crossgrain cuts 7″ wide

"We must take time to enjoy the precious moments of each day."

VICTORIAN SILKS. 54″ x 54″. Pieced and quilted by Ann Seely, 1990.

VICTORIAN SILKS
DIRECTIONS:

Use ¼" seams throughout. Refer to *General Directions*, page 12, for specific piecing information. Refer to quilt diagram, color photo, and piecing diagrams for order of assembly.

1. Place B in the lower left hand corner of A (foundation square) and baste in place. Place C right sides together along the right edge of the small square and stitch. Finger-press open. Continue in the same way with D, D, and E as illustrated.

2. Following block diagram, stitch 4 quarter blocks together to make one 6" block.

3. Lay quilt blocks out following quilt diagram. Stitch blocks into rows; stitch rows together. Trim the 4 corners to a slightly rounded shape.

4. Following the diagram for embroidery, do the embroidery in each square. Notice that where 2 small squares meet, there is a diagonal stitch across the seam.

5. Stitch the short ends of the ruffle strips together into a complete loop. Fold the ruffle wrong sides together, raw edges even. Pin pleats (approx. ½" deep and 1" apart) into the ruffle, and adjust to fit the quilt top. Allow a little extra fabric in the pleats that go around the corner curves. Baste the ruffle in place, raw edges of quilt even with raw edges of ruffle.

6. Piece backing to measure 1" to 2" larger than quilt top on each side. Center quilt top over backing, right sides together. Ruffle will be on the inside between backing and top. Pin edges and stitch, leaving an 8" opening on one side for turning. Trim backing to same size as quilt top.

7. Turn the quilt right side out and handstitch the opening closed.

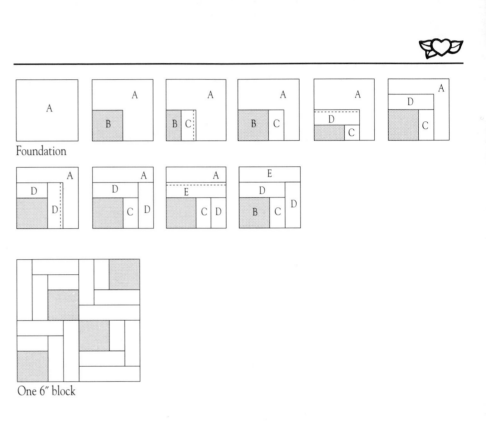

Foundation

One 6" block

Embroidery Guide

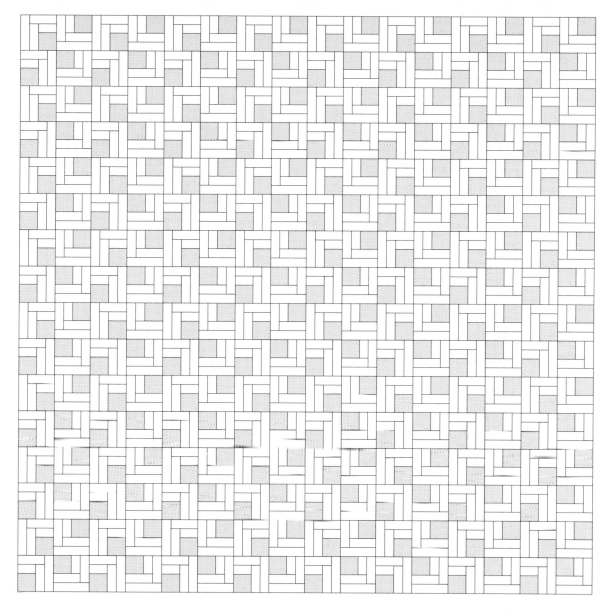

VICTORIAN SILKS – 54″ x 54″ – 6″ block – 64 blocks set 8 x 8

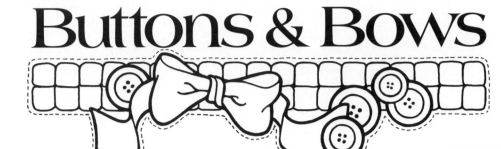

Buttons & Bows

APPROXIMATE SIZE: 49″ x 49″
BLOCK SIZE: 5″ checkerboard block and 7″ ribbon block
SETTING: 9 checkerboard blocks set straight with 12 plain blocks make up the center - 16 ribbon blocks and 4 heart applique blocks make up the border
TECHNIQUES: Patchwork, applique

"Love means giving someone your undivided attention."

YARDAGE (42″- 45″ or 107-114 cm wide):

Light pink	⅝ yd. (.6 m)
Medium pink	⅝ yd. (.6 m)
White	1⅝ yds. (1.5 m)
Dark blue	⅝ yd. (.6 m)
Light green	¼ yd. (.3 m)
Medium green	¼ yd. (.3 m)
Yellow	¼ yd. (.3 m)
Peach	¼ yd. (.3 m)
Lavender	¼ yd. (.3 m)
Light blue	¼ yd. (.3 m)
Binding	½ yd. (.5 m)
Backing	3⅛ yds. (2.9 m)
Batting (packaged)	72″ x 90″

CUTTING (Templates on pages 78 - 80):
Ar (Br, Cr, etc.) refers to A (B, C, etc.) reversed.

Light pink	Template A: 16
	Template C: 64
	Template D: 16
	Template Dr: 16
Medium pink	Template A: 64
	Template B: 32
	Template E: 16
	Template Er: 16
White	Template A: 64
	Template B: 160
	Template C: 32
	Template F: 16
	Template G: 16
	Template Gr: 16
	Template H: 12

Continued on page 105

BUTTONS AND BOWS. 49″ x 49″. Designed, pieced, and quilted by Ann Seely, 1992.

BUTTONS AND BOWS
DIRECTIONS:

Use ¼″ seams throughout. Refer to *General Directions*, page 12, for specific piecing, applique, quilting, and binding information. Refer to quilt diagram, color photo, and piecing diagrams for order of assembly.

1. Using Template I, make 9 sixteen-patch checkerboard blocks with random placement of pastel fabrics. Follow diagram and sew the checkerboard blocks and alternating plain 5½″ pastel squares to form center of quilt.

2. Applique the small pastel hearts (K) on 4 of the 5½″ pastel squares. Bottom of heart points to side of square.

3. Stitch 25½″ white borders to sides of quilt; stitch 29″ white borders to top and bottom of quilt.

4. Stitch 29½″ dark blue borders to sides of quilt; stitch 31½″ dark blue borders to top and bottom of quilt.

5. Make 16 pieced ribbon blocks following diagram.

6. Applique a light blue heart (J) on each of the 7½″ white squares. Bottom of heart points to corner of square.

7. Make 4 border units of 4 pieced ribbon blocks and 3 Template H as illustrated. Stitch border units to opposite sides of quilt, making sure bottom tips of ribbons point in toward quilt center. Stitch a large heart applique block to each end of the remaining 2 border units, making sure bottom tips of hearts point the same direction as ends of ribbons. Stitch these border units to top and bottom of quilt, making sure bottom tips of hearts and ends of ribbons point in toward quilt center.

8. Stitch 45½″ dark blue borders to sides of quilt. Stitch 49½″ dark blue borders to top and bottom of quilt.

9. Refer to *Finishing Steps For All Quilts*, page 12.

10. Quilt is hand quilted on and around both large and small heart appliques (see pattern pieces). Small hearts are quilted in the 5″ squares in the center of the quilt (see Template K). Checkerboards are ditch quilted. A scallop is quilted in the narrow white border (pattern on page 79). Ribbon blocks are quilted ⅛″ outside pink.

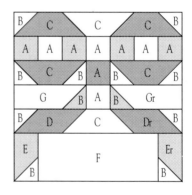

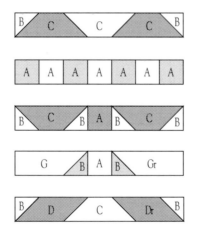

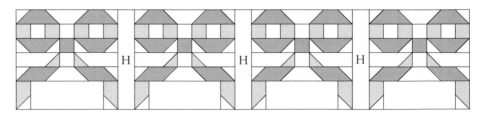

BUTTONS AND BOWS – 49″ x 49″ – 5″ checkerboard block,
7″ ribbon block – 9 checkerboard blocks, 16 ribbon blocks

Bright Colors

APPROXIMATE SIZE: 36″ x 36″
BLOCK SIZE: 8″ - 9 blocks set 3 x 3
SETTING: Blocks set straight with patchwork borders
TECHNIQUES: Patchwork

YARDAGE (42″- 45″ or 107-114 cm wide):

Dark yellow	½ yd. (.5 m)
Medium yellow	⅝ yd. (.6 m)
Light yellow	¾ yd. (.7 m)
Colored scraps	to total 1 yd. (1 m)
Binding	⅜ yd. (.4 m)
Backing	1¼ yds. (1.2 m)
Batting (packaged)	45″ x 60″
(45″ wide)	1¼ yds. (1.2 m)

CUTTING (Templates on page 80):

Dark yellow	Template B: 68
	Template C: 4
	Template A: 4
Medium yellow	Template B: 32
	Template C: 32
Light yellow	Template B: 24
	Template C: 12
	Border 2: four crossgrain cuts 2½″ x 28½″
Colored scraps	Template B: 196
	Template A: 8
Binding	4 crossgrain cuts 2½″ wide

"To make the day bright, listen to the laughter of a child."

BRIGHT COLORS. 36″ x 36″. Designed, pieced, and quilted by Ann Seely, 1992.

BRIGHT COLORS
DIRECTIONS:

Use ¼" seams throughout. Refer to *General Directions*, page 12, for specific piecing, quilting, and binding information. Refer to quilt diagram, color photo, and piecing diagrams for order of assembly.

1. Using dark yellow as the background color, make 1 block as illustrated.

2. Using medium yellow as the background color, make 8 more blocks.

3. Set the blocks together in 3 rows of 3 with the dark yellow block in the middle of the center row.

4. Border 1: Using light yellow, make 4 border rows following the diagram. Sew border rows to 2 opposite sides of the quilt. Add a colored square (A) to each end of the 2 remaining border rows. Sew these border rows to the top and bottom of the quilt.

5. Border 2: Sew 28½" strips of light yellow to 2 opposite sides of the quilt. Add a colored square (A) to each end of the 2 remaining light yellow strips and sew these borders to the top and bottom of the quilt.

6. Border 3: Using dark yellow as the background color, make 4 patchwork strips for border 3 following the diagram. Notice that the triangles reverse directions in the center of each border. Sew border rows to two opposite sides of the quilt following diagram. Add a dark yellow square (A) to each end of the 2 remaining borders and sew these border rows to the top and bottom of the quilt.

7. Refer to *Finishing Steps For All Quilts*, page 12.

8. Quilt is hand quilted in the ditch between the bright solid triangles. Five double hearts are quilted in each light yellow border, pattern on page 80. Squares set on point are quilted in the medium yellow background.

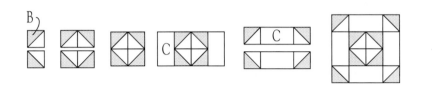

Make 4 patchwork strips for Border 1

Make 4 patchwork strips for Border 3

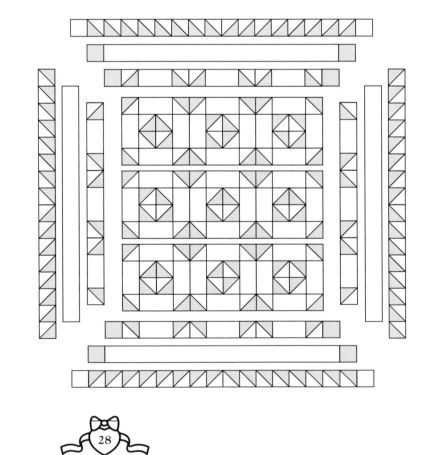

28

BRIGHT COLORS – 36″ x 36″ – 8″ block – 9 blocks set 3 x 3

Roses For Sue

APPROXIMATE SIZE: 43″ x 49″

BLOCK SIZE: 8½″ x 10½″- 9 blocks set 3 x 3

SETTING: Blocks set with pieced sashing and framed by a border of small squares

TECHNIQUES: Patchwork, applique, embroidery

"Childhood is a time to store up happy memories."

YARDAGE (42″- 45″ or 107-114 cm wide):

Patchwork fabrics:

Cream (background & border)	1¼ yds. (1.2 m)
Medium floral (border squares)	½ yd. (.5 m)
Large floral (sashing)	½ yd. (.5 m)
Dark pink (border squares)	½ yd. (.5 m)
Medium pink (border squares)	¼ yd. (.3 m)
Dark green (border squares)	⅓ yd. (.3 m)
Medium green (border squares)	¼ yd. (.3 m)
Black (sashing)	½ yd. (.5 m)

Applique fabrics:

Dress	6″ x 7″ (9)
Blouse & sleeve	4″ x 4″ (9)
Hat	5″ x 5″ (9)
Basket	3″ x 3″ (9)
Pantaloon	2″ x 3″ (9)
Shoe	2″ x 3″ (9)
Arms	3″ x 3″ (9)
Binding	½ yd. (.5 m)
Backing	3 yds. (2.8 m)
Batting (packaged)	45″ x 60″
Purchased ribbon roses	18
Green embroidery thread	1 skein

CUTTING (Templates on page 81):

Applique:

Cream (bkgrnd.)	9″ x 11″ (cut 9)
Arm	Templates A, G: 9 each
Blouse	Template B: 9
Sleeve	Template H: 9
Foot	Template C: 9
Pantaloon	Template D: 9
Dress	Template E: 9

Continued on page 105

ROSES FOR SUE. 43″ x 49″. Designed, pieced, and quilted by Joyce Stewart, 1992.
Sue block designed by Shari Jo Shirley.

ROSES FOR SUE

DIRECTIONS:

Use ¼″ seams throughout. Refer to *General Directions*, page 12, for specific piecing, applique, quilting, and binding information. Refer to quilt diagram, color photo, and piecing diagrams for order of assembly.

1. Applique Sue on the background blocks in order from A to I.

2. Sew a rose above Sue's right hand. Embroider the stems with green embroidery thread using a stem stitch. Sew roses to baskets.

3. Sew ¾″ black sashing strips to each side of the 1½″ large-floral sashing strips (side sashing strips are longer than tops and bottoms). Sew long sashing strips to sides of applique blocks to make 3 rows of 3 girls. Sew small black squares to short sashes to make 4 rows. See diagrams.

4. Assemble 4 rows of sashing and 3 rows of applique, referring to quilt diagram and color photo.

5. Make patchwork border:
   a. Make 4 corner units, 2 side units, and 2 top/bottom units, as illustrated, with the 2″ squares (Template J).
   b. Stitch side units to opposite sides of quilt; make sure the side of the border with the cream squares in it is next to the quilt.
   c. Stitch corner units to each end of the top and bottom border units; make sure color placement is correct by referring to diagrams and color photo. Stitch to top and bottom of quilt making sure the side of each border unit with the cream squares in it is next to the quilt.

6. Refer to *Finishing Steps For All Quilts*, page 12.

7. Quilt is hand quilted in a 1¼″ diagonal crosshatch pattern in the background of the appliques. A line of quilting outlines each applique piece.

The sashing is quilted in the ditch, and an X is quilted in each black square. The border is quilted in diagonal lines through the corners of some of the patchwork squares.

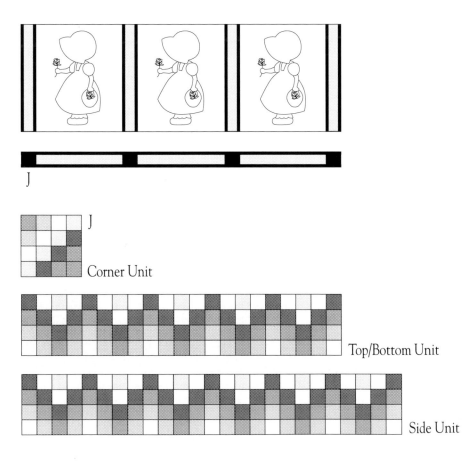

J

Corner Unit

Top/Bottom Unit

Side Unit

ROSES FOR SUE – 43″ x 49″ – 8½″ x 10½″ block – 9 blocks set 3 x 3

Teddy Bears On Parade

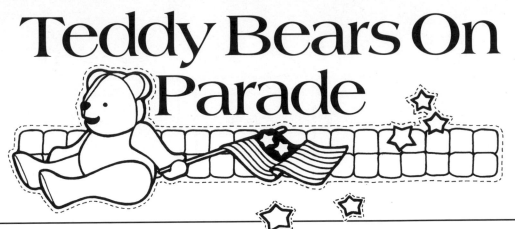

APPROXIMATE SIZE: 39″ x 30″
BLOCK SIZE: 4½″ - 24 blocks
SETTING: Blocks set around applique center
TECHNIQUES: Patchwork and applique;
embellished with purchased flags

YARDAGE (42″- 45″ or 107-114 cm wide):

Cream (applique background)	⅜ yd. (.4 m)
Red stripe (floor)	¾ yd. (.7 m)
	(¼ yd. if not a stripe) (.3 m)
Dark brown scraps (bears)	5″ x 7″ (3)
Medium brown scraps (bears)	6″ x 10″ (3)
Light brown scraps (bears)	3½″ x 4″ (3)
Dark blue (borders)	½ yd. (.5 m)
Red (star points)	⅝ yd. (.6 m)
White (star background)	⅞ yd. (.8 m)
Light blue (star patchwork)	¼ yd. (.3 m)
Binding	⅜ yd. (.4 m)
Backing	1 yd. (1 m)
Batting (packaged)	45″ x 60″
(45″ wide)	1 yd. (1 m)
Fabric flags with poles - 4″ x 6″	3

CUTTING (Templates on page 82):
Ar (Br, Cr, etc.) refers to A (B, C, etc.) reversed.

Cream	11″ x 24½″ (cut 1)
Red stripe	5″ x 24½″ (cut 1)
Dark brown scraps	Templates F, G, H: 3 each
Medium brown scraps	Templates I, J, K, L: 3 each
Light brown scraps	Template E: 3
Dark blue	
Inside border	2″ x 18½″ (cut 2)
	2″ x 24½″ (cut 2)
Outside border	2″ x 30½″ (cut 2)
	2″ x 36½″ (cut 2)
Light blue	Template A: 144
White	Template A: 144
	Template C: 96
	Template D: 48
Red	Templates B, Br: 96 each
Binding	4 crossgrain cuts 2½″ wide

*"The more we love, the more our
ability to love increases."*

TEDDY BEARS ON PARADE. 39″ x 30″. Designed, pieced, and quilted by Ann Seely, 1991.

TEDDY BEARS ON PARADE
DIRECTIONS:

Use ¼" seams throughout. Refer to *General Directions*, page 12, for specific piecing, applique, quilting, and binding information. Refer to quilt diagram, color photo, and piecing diagrams for order of assembly.

1. Stitch applique background to floor. Press seam toward floor.

2. Position bears using bear pattern on page 82 and the photo as guides. Applique bears to background, leaving right arm open as indicated on pattern for inserting purchased flags. Applique order: left ear, arm, and leg; body; head; right ear, arm, and leg. Optional: Stuff bears' arms, legs, and head by cutting small slits in the background fabric behind each applique piece and stuffing lightly with small amounts of batting.

3. Stitch inside border to top, bottom, and sides, in that order.

4. Make 24 pieced blocks following piecing diagrams.

5. Make 4 panels of 6 blocks each as illustrated.

6. Stitch panels to top, bottom, and sides of applique panel, in that order. Refer to quilt diagram and photo.

7. Stitch outside border to top, bottom, and sides of quilt in that order.

8. Insert flag sticks into openings in bears' hands. Arrange flags as desired and applique edges to quilt top.

9. Refer to *Finishing Steps For All Quilts*, page 12.

10. Applique section of quilt is hand quilted next to bears and flags; parallel lines are quilted on the floor; a starburst pattern radiates outward from each bear. A bow is quilted in the inner border, pattern on page 82. The star patchwork border is outline quilted, and a quilting line is added diagonally through the light blue squares. The outer border is quilted with a single zig-zag line.

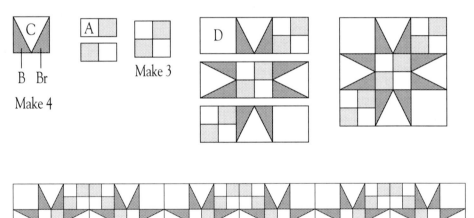

TEDDY BEARS ON PARADE – 39″ x 30″ – 4½″ block – 24 blocks set around applique center

Pinwheels & Posies

APPROXIMATE SIZE: 62″ x 94″

BLOCK SIZE: 6″ - 40 blocks set 5 x 8

SETTING: Pinwheel blocks set straight with pieced sashing containing Nine-patch blocks

TECHNIQUES: Patchwork

YARDAGE (42″- 45″ or 107-114 cm wide):

Light floral	3 yds. (2.8 m)
Dark floral	3 yds. (2.8 m)
Blue	1¼ yds. (1.2 m)
Pink	2½ yds. (2.3 m)
Binding	¾ yd. (.7 m)
Backing	5¾ yds. (5.3 m)
Batting (packaged)	81″ x 96″
(45″ wide)	5¾ yds. (5.3 m)

CUTTING (Templates on page 83):

Light floral	Template A: 160
	Template B: 160
Dark floral	Template B: 67
	Template C: 188
	Border 2: 2 lengthwise grain strips 4½″ x 66″
	2 lengthwise grain strips 4½″ x 98″
Blue	Template A: 160
	Template C: 4
Pink	Template C: 134
	Border 1: 2 lengthwise grain strips 2″ x 51½″
	2 lengthwise grain strips 2″ x 83″
Binding	8 crossgrain cuts 2½″ wide

"It is easier to grow old than it is to grow up."

PINWHEELS AND POSIES. *62″ x 94″. Designed, pieced, and quilted by Joyce Stewart, 1992.*

PINWHEELS AND POSIES
DIRECTIONS:

Use ¼″ seams throughout. Refer to *General Directions*, page 12, for specific piecing, quilting, and binding information. Refer to quilt diagram, color photo, and piecing diagrams for order of assembly.

1. Make 40 Pinwheel blocks following diagram.
2. Make 67 Unit 1 following diagram.
3. Make 8 Pinwheel rows as illustrated.
4. Make 28 Nine-patch blocks as illustrated.
5. Make 22 Unit 2 as illustrated.
6. Make 7 Nine-patch rows following diagram.
7. Stitch Pinwheel rows and Nine-patch rows together, beginning and ending with a Pinwheel row.
8. Make 2 finishing rows as illustrated. Stitch finishing rows to top and bottom of quilt.
9. Stitch 83″ Border 1 strips to sides of quilt.
10. Stitch a blue C to each end of the 51½″ Border 1 strips. Stitch Border 1 to top and bottom of quilt.
11. Stitch Border 2 strips to sides, top, and bottom of quilt, following directions given in mitered borders section of *General Directions*, page 14.
12. Refer to *Finishing Steps For All Quilts*, page 12.
13. Quilt is machine quilted in the ditch between patches and hand quilted in the border in a 2½″ crosshatch pattern. Centers of pinwheels are stitched down by machine in an X.

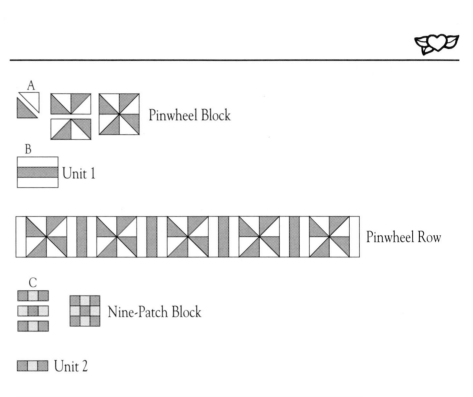

A   Pinwheel Block

B   Unit 1

Pinwheel Row

C   Nine-Patch Block

Unit 2

Nine-Patch Row

Finishing Row

PINWHEELS AND POSIES – 62″ x 94″ – 6″ block – 40 blocks set 5 x 8

Sweet Sixteen

APPROXIMATE SIZE: 40″ x 40″
SETTING: Sixteen hearts with ribbons appliqued on a whole-cloth background
TECHNIQUES: Applique

YARDAGE (42″- 45″ or 107-114 cm wide):

Navy background	1¼ yds. (1.2 m)
Very light pink	¼ yd. (.3 m)
Light pink	¼ yd. (.3 m)
Medium pink	¼ yd. (.3 m)
Dark pink	¼ yd. (.3 m)
Very light aqua	⅛ yd. (.2 m)
Light aqua	¼ yd. (.3 m)
Medium aqua	⅜ yd. (.4 m)
Medium-dark aqua	¼ yd. (.3 m)
Dark aqua	⅜ yd. (.4 m)
Binding	½ yd. (.5 m)
Backing	1¼ yds. (1.2 m)
Batting (packaged)	45″ x 60″
(45″ wide)	1¼ yds. (1.2 m)

CUTTING (Templates on pages 84, 85):
Ar (Br, Cr, etc.) refers to A (B, C, etc.) reversed.

Navy bkgrnd.	42″ x 42″
Very light pink	Template A: 4
Light pink	Template A: 4
Med. pink	Template A: 4
Dark pink	Template A: 4
Very light aqua	Templates G, I, J: 4 each
Light aqua	Templates Cr, Dr, Fr, H, K: 4 each
Med. aqua	Templates Br, Er, Gr, Ir, Jr, L, Lr, M, Mr: 4 each
	Template Q: 8
Med-dark aqua	Templates C, D, F, Hr, Kr: 4 each
Dark aqua	Templates B, E, N, Nr, O, Or, R: 4 each
	Template P: 8
Binding	5 crossgrain cuts 2½″ wide

"Because I love today, I am not afraid to face tomorrow."

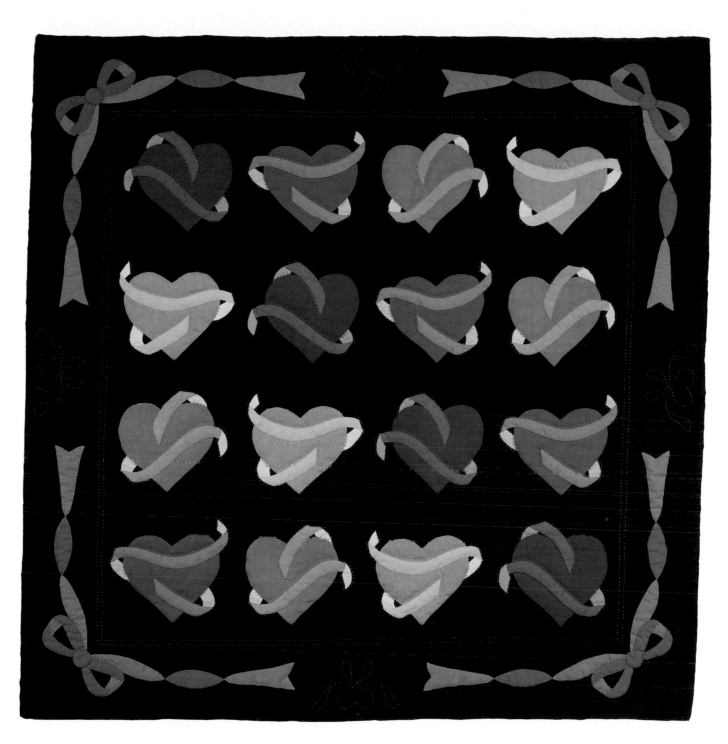

SWEET SIXTEEN. 40″ x 40″. Designed and appliqued by Joyce Stewart; quilted by Ann Seely, 1992. Quilting design in border is given with permission from *Quilter's Newsletter Magazine*.

SWEET SIXTEEN
DIRECTIONS:

Use ¼″ seams throughout. Refer to *General Directions*, page 12, for specific applique, quilting, and binding information. Refer to quilt diagram, color photo, and piecing diagrams for placement.

1. On the 42″ x 42″ background, thread-mark, with a basting stitch, 7½″ squares and a 5″ border. Do not trim to finished size until applique is finished.

2. Refer to color photo and heart diagrams for color placement of applique pieces. Applique hearts, ribbons, and bows using photo as a guide for placement.

3. Remove basting stitches. Trim sides of quilt top, leaving an even border, to 40″ x 40″.

4. Refer to *Finishing Steps For All Quilts*, page 12.

5. Quilt is quilted in a 1¼″ grid by hand in the center between the heart appliques; all appliques are defined by a quilting line ⅛″ outside the edges of each piece. Two rows of quilting ¼″ apart define the center of the quilt from the border area, and the border area is quilted in diagonal parallel lines 1″ apart. Quilting pattern for center of border is on page 84.

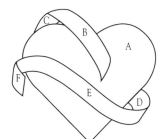

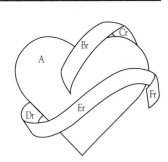

Heart #1
Dark pink: A
Med-dark aqua: C, D, F
Dark aqua: B, E

Heart #2
Light pink: A
Light aqua: Cr, Dr, Fr
Medium aqua: Br, Er

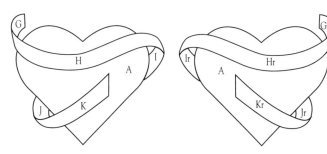

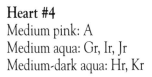

Heart #3
Very light pink: A
Very light aqua: G, I, J
Light aqua: H, K

Heart #4
Medium pink: A
Medium aqua: Gr, Ir, Jr
Medium-dark aqua: Hr, Kr

SWEET SIXTEEN – 40″ x 40″ – 16 hearts with ribbons appliqued on a whole-cloth background

Duet

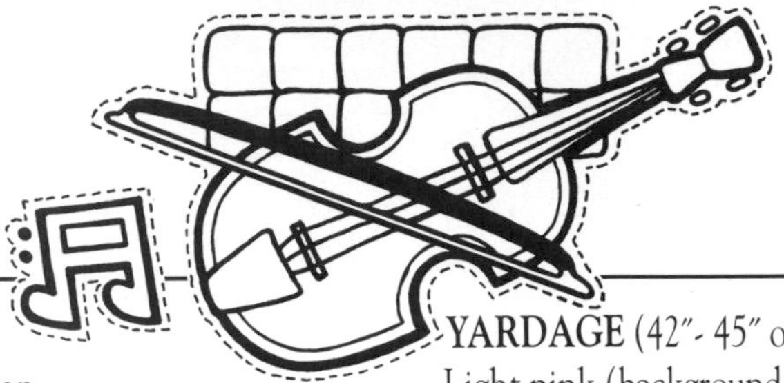

APPROXIMATE SIZE: 91″ x 91″
BLOCK SIZE: 17¼″ central medallion,
10″ border block (24)
SETTING: Medallion
TECHNIQUES: Patchwork, applique

*"To make the woods a joyful place, we
must each sing our own song."*

YARDAGE (42″- 45″ or 107-114 cm wide):

Light pink (background)	2½ yds. (2.3 m)
Turquoise stripe (outside border)	3 yds. (2.8 m)
	(need 4 repeats of a stripe
	that can be cut 9¼″ wide)

Mariner's Compass:

Narrow turquoise stripe (frame)	¾ yd. (.7 m)
Dark green	¼ yd. (.3 m)
Black floral	¼ yd. (.3 m)
Medium dark turquoise	¼ yd. (.3 m)
Light turquoise	¼ yd. (.3 m)
Tan	⅛ yd. (.2 m)
Black	⅛ yd. (.2 m)
Gray	⅛ yd. (.2 m)
Pink print	4″ x 4″

Ribbon Border:

Dark pink	½ yd. (.5 m)
Dark turquoise print	⅝ yd. (.6 m)
Turquoise solid	½ yd. (.5 m)

Pieced Block Border:

Pink print	1⅛ yds. (1.1 m)
Turquoise print	1 yd. (1 m)
Cream	1 yd. (1 m)
Dark green	¾ yd. (.7 m)
Gray	⅝ yd. (.7 m)
Binding	1 yd. (1 m)
Backing	8½ yds. (7.8 m)
Batting (packaged)	120″ x 120″
(45″ wide)	8¼ yds. (7.6 m)

CUTTING (Templates on pages 86 - 91):
Ar (Br, Cr, etc.) refers to A (B, C, etc.) reversed.
Mariner's Compass:

Pink print	Template M: 1

Continued on page 106

DUET. 91″ x 91″. Designed, pieced, and quilted by Ann Seely, 1990. Quilting design in light pink border is from *Dear Helen, Can You Tell Me?...all about quilting designs.* by Helen Squire, American Quilter's Society.

DUET

DIRECTIONS:

Use ¼″ seams throughout. Refer to *General Directions*, page 12, for specific applique, piecing, quilting, and binding information. Refer to quilt diagram, color photo, and piecing diagrams for placement.

1. Make Mariner's Compass: Applique the pink print circle (Template M) to the gray circle (Template N). Follow the chart for piecing the small compass and applique it to the gray circle (Template O). Follow the diagram for piecing the large compass and applique it to the 17¾″ light pink square.

2. Add the turquoise border to the compass block following the directions for mitered borders in the *General Directions* section, page 14. Cut the 16⅝″ light pink squares in half diagonally and sew the long edges of the resulting triangles to the sides of the compass block.

3. Add the dark pink border following the directions for mitered borders.

4. Referring to diagrams on page 106, make the ribbon border: Make 2 short units using A, B, and C as illustrated. Make 2 long units (including corners) using Ar, B, C, D, E, F, Fr, G, and H as illustrated. Stitch the 2 short units *to* opposite sides of the quilt, making sure the pink C's are facing the quilt; stitch the 2 long units to the top and bottom of the quilt. Stitch diagonal seams at corners.

5. Stitch the light pink border strips to the gray border strips and stitch them as a unit to the quilt, then follow the directions for mitered borders.

6. Make 24 pieced blocks following the diagram. Make 2 rows of 5 blocks and stitch them to the sides of the quilt. Make 2 rows of 7 blocks and stitch them to top and bottom of quilt.

7. Add the gray border following the directions for mitered borders .

8. Stitch the turquoise stripe border to the quilt following the directions mitered borders.

9. Refer to *Finishing Steps For All Quilts*, page 12.

10. Quilt is ditch quilted by hand in Mariner's Compass and outline quilted around it. A feather quilting pattern, page 89, is used between the medallion center and the ribbon border, A leaf motif pattern on page 90, is used in the border between the ribbon and block borders. Blocks are double-line quilted in arcs through the cream diamonds. Outer border is quilted along lines in the stripe. A small motif, page 91, is quilted in each corner of the Mariner's Compass block.

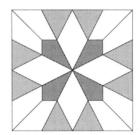

DUET – 91″ x 91″ – 17¼″ central medallion, 10″ border block

Friendship Basket

APPROXIMATE SIZE: 77″ x 93″

BLOCK SIZE: 10″ - 32 blocks set 4 x 5

SETTING: Basket blocks set on point with narrow sashing

TECHNIQUES: Patchwork blocks signed with permanent ink marker

YARDAGE (42″- 45″ or 107-114 cm wide):

Muslin	1½ yds. (1.4 m)
Dark blue (sashing)	2⅛ yds. (2 m)
Light green (sashing, border)	1⅞ yds. (1.8 m)
Medium prints	to total 4 yds. (3.7 m)
Light prints	to total 2½ yds. (2.3 m)
Binding	⅞ yd. (.8 m)
Backing	5⅝ yds. (5.2 m)
Batting (packaged)	81″ x 96″
(45″ wide)	5½ yds. (5.1 m)
Permanent ink marker	

CUTTING (Templates on pages 91 - 95):

Ar (Br, Cr, etc.) refers to A (B, C, etc.) reversed.

For each block:

Muslin	Template A: 1
Medium print	Template A: 1
	Template D: 8
Light print	Template B: 2
	Templates C, E: 1 each
	Template D: 6

Setting triangles and sashings:

Muslin	Template F: 14
Medium print	Template G: 14
	Template I: 4
Dark blue	Template H: 14
	Template J: 8
	Template K: 66
	Templates L, M: 4 each
	Template Mr: 6
Light green	Template N: 31
	Border: 9 crossgrain cuts 6″ wide
Binding	9 crossgrain cuts 3″ wide

"By signing a friendship quilt, we are held together by shared memories."

FRIENDSHIP BASKET. *77" x 93".* Designed and pieced by Joyce Stewart,
quilted by LaRae Mackay, 1990-1992. Owned by Jim and Shari Jo Shirley.

51

FRIENDSHIP BASKET
DIRECTIONS:

Use ¼″ seams throughout. Refer to *General Directions*, page 12, for specific piecing, quilting, and binding information. Refer to quilt diagram, color photo, and piecing diagrams for order of assembly.

1. Make 32 basket blocks following piecing diagrams. Have friends sign the muslin triangles with a permanent ink marker.

2. Make 14 setting triangles for the sides as illustrated. Sew Templates F and G together and add Template H. These may also be signed.

3. Make 4 setting triangles for the corners. Sew Template J to I and add J.

4. Refer to diagram for constructing the diagonal rows of blocks and setting triangles. Sew the rows together as illustrated.

5. Add the light green border, referring to directions for mitered borders in *General Directions* section, page 14.

6. Refer to *Finishing Steps For All Quilts*, page 12. Use a ½″ seam allowance to attach binding.

7. Quilt is hand quilted in the ditch between patches in the blocks. Other quilting lines in the blocks are shown in the quilting guide diagram. Freeform hearts and curved lines are quilted around the signatures. Ditch quilting is done between blocks and sashing. A swag quilting design, pattern on page 93, is used in the border.

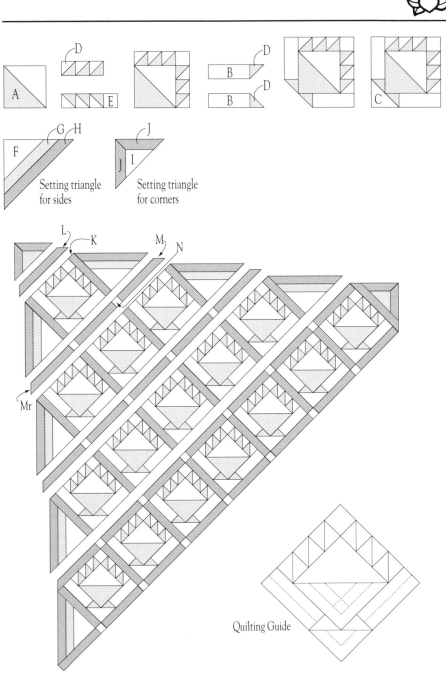

Setting triangle for sides

Setting triangle for corners

Quilting Guide

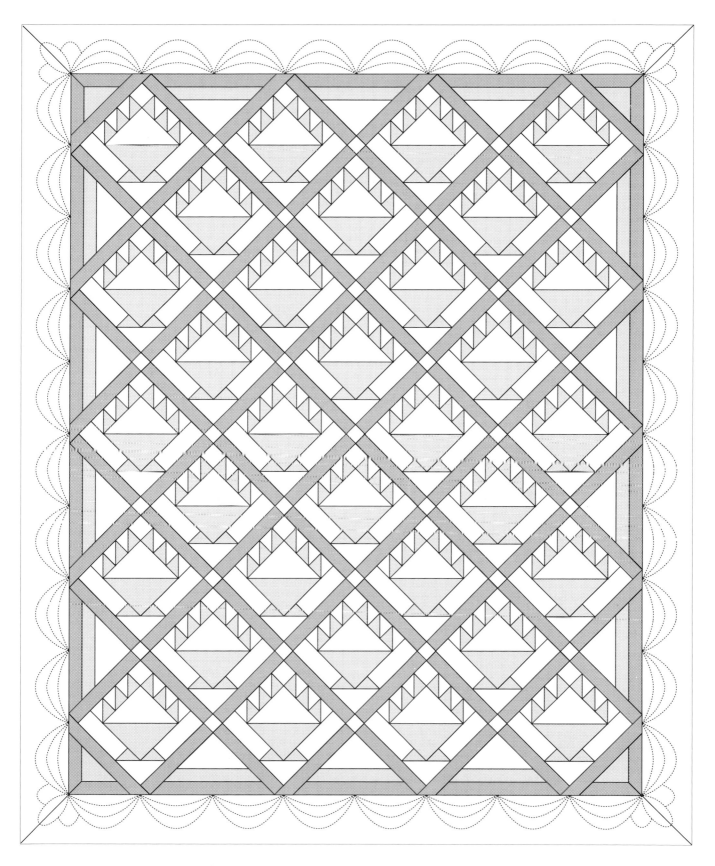

FRIENDSHIP BASKET – 77″ x 93″ – 10″ block – 32 blocks set 4 x 5 on point

Bride's Bouquet

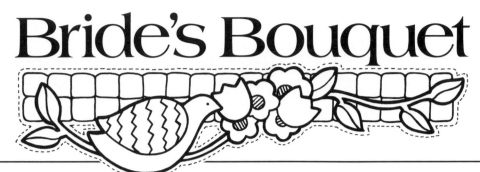

APPROXIMATE SIZE: 28″ x 29″
SETTING: Appliqued bouquet with border
TECHNIQUES: Applique, satin ribbon attached with beads

"We do not love people because they are beautiful; they are beautiful to us because we love them."

YARDAGE (42″- 45″ or 107-114 cm wide):

White (background)	⅝ yd. (.6 m)
Pink floral (borders)	⅝ yd. (.6 m)
Green (stems and leaves)	⅜ yd. (.4 m)
Greens (leaves)	9″ x 9″ (2)
Light blue solid (small bird, flowers)	⅛ yd. (.2 m)
Light blue print (wing)	⅛ yd. (.2 m)
Medium blue solid (large bird)	⅙ yd. (.2 m)
Medium blue print (wing)	⅛ yd. (.2 m)
Medium pink solid (heart)	8″ x 8″
Dark pink print (flowers)	4″x 8″
Light yellows (flowers)	4″ x 4″ (2)
Yellow prints (flower centers)	2″ x 2″ (2)
Orange (tulips)	4″x 8″
Light pink solid (flowers & centers)	4″ x 18″
Light pink print (flower centers)	2″ x 4″
Dark pink solid (flower & center)	6″ x 9″
Medium pink print (flower)	4″ x 4″
1″ wide pink satin ribbon	1½ yds. (1.4 m)
5mm pearl beads	approx. 24
Bias bars	⅜″, ½″, ⅝″
Binding	⅓ yd. (.3 m)
Backing	1 yd. (1 m)
Batting (packaged)	36″ x 45″
(45″ wide)	1 yd. (1 m)

CUTTING (Templates on pages 94, 95):
Ar (Br, Cr, etc.) refers to A (B, C, etc.) reversed.

White	18½″ square (cut 1)
Pink floral	5½″ x 18½″ (cut 2)
	5½″ x 28½″ (cut 1)
	6½″ x 28½″ (cut 1)

Continued on page 105

BRIDE'S BOUQUET. 28″ x 29″. Designed, pieced, appliqued, and quilted by Ann Seely, 1992.

BRIDE'S BOUQUET

DIRECTIONS:

Use ¼″ seams throughout. Refer to *General Directions*, page 12, for specific applique, piecing, quilting, and binding information. Refer to quilt diagram, color photo, and piecing diagrams for order of assembly.

1. Applique the stems, leaves and flowers of the central bouquet, in that order, to the white square. Refer to applique diagram and color photo for placement.

2. Sew the 5½″ x 18½″ borders to the sides of the center square. Sew the 5½″ x 28½″ border to the top and the 6½″ x 28½″ border to the bottom.

3. Complete the applique at each side of the central motif: Applique the stems cut 1¾″ to the lower half of the quilt top and the stems cut 1½″ to the upper half of the quilt top, curving the upper stems. The raw ends of the stems will be covered by other applique pieces. Applique the birds and leaves. Applique the dark pink print flowers to cover the raw ends where the wide and narrow stems meet. Center the large pink heart in the lower border and applique.

4. Tie a loose bow in the satin ribbon. Twist and fold the ribbon as desired and pin in place. Sew a pearl bead at each pinned fold.

5. Refer to *Finishing Steps For All Quilts*, page 12.

6. Quilt is hand quilted around the appliques, in a double-line crosshatch pattern in the cream background, and in ¾″ parallel lines in the border. Quilting design for large heart is included on the pattern piece.

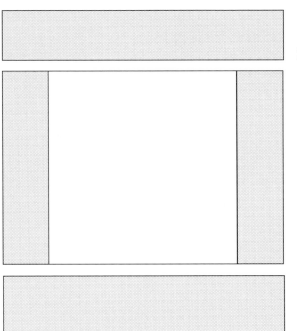

5½″ x 28½″ piece

6½″ x 28½″ piece

BRIDE'S BOUQUET – 28″ x 29″ – appliqued bouquet with border

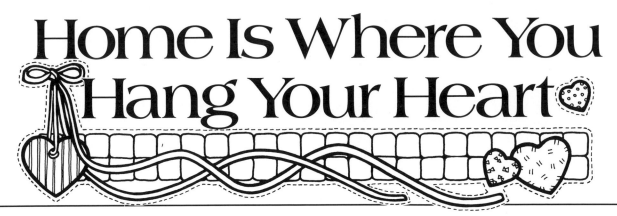

Home Is Where You Hang Your Heart

APPROXIMATE SIZE: 23″ x 23″
BLOCK SIZE: 6¼″ - 4 blocks set 2 x 2
SETTING: Blocks set straight with sashing and borders
TECHNIQUES: Patchwork, applique, embellished with silk cording

YARDAGE (42″- 45″ or 107-114 cm wide):

Cream (background)	⅓ yd. (.3 m)
Light blue (houses)	four 7″ x 7″ scraps
Navy blue (roofs, chimneys)	four 7″ x 7″ scraps
Red (hearts)	four 4″ x 4″ scraps
Green (grass)	four 3″ x 8″ scraps
Medium blue (sashings)	⅙ yd. (.2 m)
Orange-red (narrow border)	⅛ yd. (.2 m)
Navy blue (checkered border)	¼ yd. (.3 m)
Light beige (checkered border)	¼ yd. (.3 m)
Red plaid (outside border)	¼ yd. (.3 m)
Binding	⅓ yd. (.3 m)
Backing	⅞ yd. (.8 m)
Batting (packaged)	45″ x 60″
(45″ wide)	¾ yd. (.7 m)
Red silk cording	1½ yds. (1.4 m)

CUTTING (Templates on page 96):

Cream	6¾″ x 6¾″ (cut 4)
Light blue	Template A: cut 4
Navy	Templates B, C: cut 4 each
Red	Template D: cut 4
Green	Template E: cut 4
Med. blue	1″ x 6¾″ (cut 2)
	1″ x 13½″ (cut 3)
	1″ x 14½″ (cut 2)
Orange-red	1″ x 14½″ (cut 2)
	1″ x 15½″ (cut 2)
Navy	3 crossgrain cuts 1½″ wide
Light beige	3 crossgrain cuts 1½″ wide
Red plaid	2″ x 19½″ (cut 2)
	2″ x 22½″ (cut 2)
Red silk cording	2½″ (cut 4)
	11″ (cut 4)
Binding	3 crossgrain cuts 2¼″ wide

"Houses are built with our hands; homes are built with our hearts."

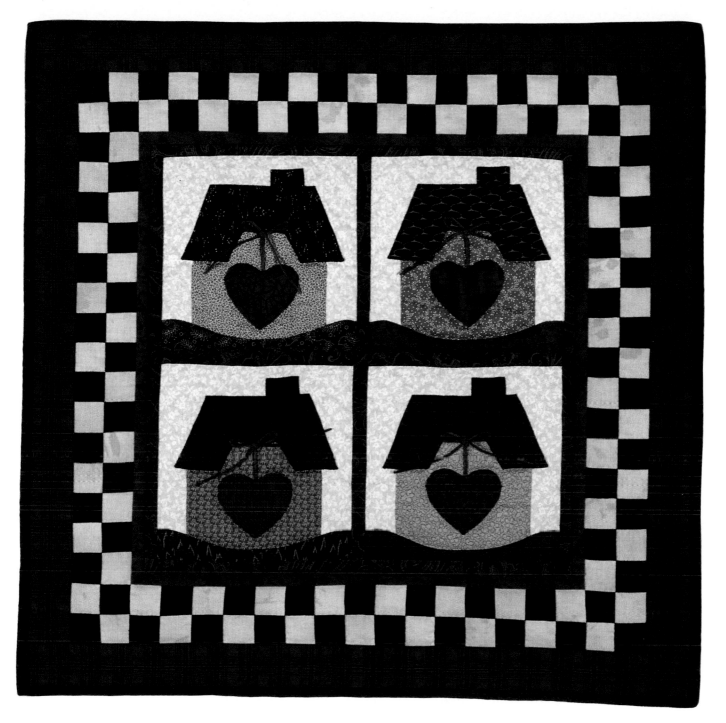

HOME IS WHERE YOU HANG YOUR HEART. *23" x 23".*
Designed, pieced, and quilted by Joyce Stewart, 1992.

HOME IS WHERE YOU HANG YOUR HEART
DIRECTIONS:

Use ¼″ seams throughout. Refer to *General Directions*, page 12, for specific applique, piecing, quilting, and binding information. Refer to quilt diagram, color photo, and piecing diagrams for order of assembly.

1. Applique the houses (Template A), then applique the 2½″ pieces of cording in place on the houses, referring to Template A for placement. Applique the chimneys, roofs, hearts, and grass.

2. Tie the 11″ pieces of cording into bows and tack them in place using the photo as a guide. Apply Fray Check™ to the ends of the cording to prevent raveling.

3. Assemble blocks with blue sashing: Stitch 2 house blocks together with 6¾″ piece of sashing. Repeat with other 2 blocks. Stitch 13½″ piece of sashing to top of one 2-block unit, then stitch bottom of other 2-block unit to the other side of the sashing strip. Stitch a 13½″ strip of sashing to each side. Stitch 14½″ strips of blue sashing to top and bottom.

4. Add orange-red border: Stitch 14½″ orange-red borders to each side of quilt; stitch 15½″ orange-red borders to top and bottom.

5. Make checkerboard borders.
   a. Stitch 1½″ strips of navy and light beige together. Press seam toward dark fabric.
   b. Cut into 1½″ segments.
   c. Stitch segments into strips, alternating direction of segments. Make 2 strips of 15 segments; make 2 strips of 19 segments.
   d. Press seams in one direction.
   e. Sew a 15½″ border to each side of quilt, then stitch 19½″ borders to top and bottom.

6. Add red plaid border: Stitch 19½″ border pieces to sides of quilt; stitch 22½″ border pieces to top and bottom.

7. Refer to *Finishing Steps For All Quilts*, page 12. Use a ¼″ seam allowance to attach binding.

8. Quilt is hand quilted in a ½″ crosshatch pattern in the block background. Appliques, sashing, narrow border, and checkered border are quilted in the ditch. A zigzag pattern is quilted in the outside border.

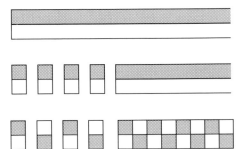

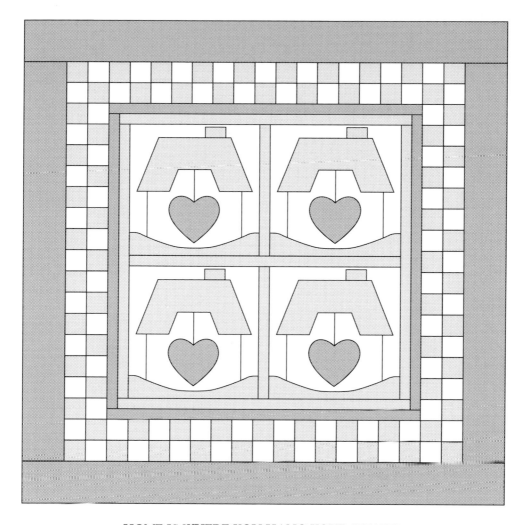

HOME IS WHERE YOU HANG YOUR HEART
23″ x 23″ – 6¼″ block – 4 blocks set 2 x 2

Nighttime Magic

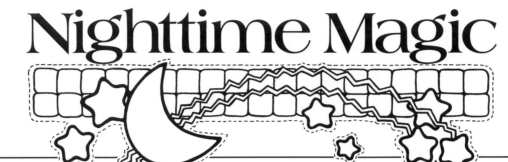

APPROXIMATE SIZE: 47″ x 47″

BLOCK SIZE: 8½″ - 9 blocks set 3 x 3

SETTING: Nine Magic Pineapple Blocks with finishing triangles set straight, surrounded by smaller blocks and framed with an applique border

TECHNIQUES: Patchwork, applique

YARDAGE (42″- 45″ or 107-114 cm wide):

Navy (patchwork, borders)	1½ yds. (1.4 m)
Greens (applique)	to total ¾ yd. (.7 m)
Pinks (applique)	to total ¾ yd. (.7 m)
Dark blue (triangles)	¾ yd. (.7 m)
Light pink (triangles)	½ yd. (.5 m)
Light green (triangles)	½ yd. (.5 m)
Greens, lts. to dks. (strips)	to total ¼ yd. (.3 m)
Pinks, lts. to dks. (strips)	to total ⅓ yd. (.3 m)
Blues, lts. to dks. (strips)	to total ⅝ yd. (.6 m)
Binding	½ yd. (.5 m)
Backing	3 yds. (2.8 m)
Batting (packaged)	72″ x 90″
Bias bar	¼″

CUTTING (Templates on pages 97, 98):

Note: Templates A and B are not marked with seamlines and are cut oversize so that if they are not placed exactly, they will still work. Also, strips for Magic Blocks are cut slightly larger than necessary for the same reason.

Navy	Template A: 9
	Template B: 108
	Borders: 4 lengthwise grain cuts 7″ x 48″
Greens (applique)	Template G: 40
	Bias strips 1″ x 4″ (cut 32)
	Bias strips 1″ x 8″ (cut 20)
Pinks (applique)	Templates D, E: 24 each
	Template F: 32
Dark blue (triangles)	Template C: 48
Light pink (triangles)	Template C: 20
Light green (triangles)	Template C: 24

Continued on page 107

"Time that you enjoy wasting is not wasted time."

NIGHTTIME MAGIC. 47″ x 47″. Designed, pieced, and quilted by Joyce Stewart, 1992.

NIGHTTIME MAGIC
DIRECTIONS:

Use ¼″ seams throughout. Refer to *General Directions*, page 12, for specific applique, piecing, quilting, and binding information. Refer to quilt diagram, color photo, and piecing diagrams for order of assembly.

1. Make 9 Magic Blocks: Make 1 block with all four sides of the block shaded from dark pink in the center to light pink at the outside edge. Make 4 blocks with all four sides of the block shaded from light blue in the center to dark blue at the outside edge. Make 4 blocks with pinks on two opposite sides, greens on one side, and blues on the other side. Pinks and greens will shade from darks in the center out to lights. Blues will shade from lights in the center out to darks.

   a. Make 9 photocopies of the full-size block on page 97. Trace each line on other side of paper (use light box or window). Use lines on traced side as a guide in placing fabrics and lines on other side as sewing lines.

   b. Place A, right side up, on center square marked on traced side of paper. Use tiny dab of glue stick to hold it in place. Place 1½″ x 2¾″ strip on A, right side down, raw edges together.

   c. *From paper side*, stitch strip and center square to paper. Extend stitching ¼″ beyond seamline. Use short stitch so paper will tear away easily when finished.

   d. Turn block over; open and press strip flat. Repeat on opposite side of center square, then on other 2 sides of center square.

Continued on page 107

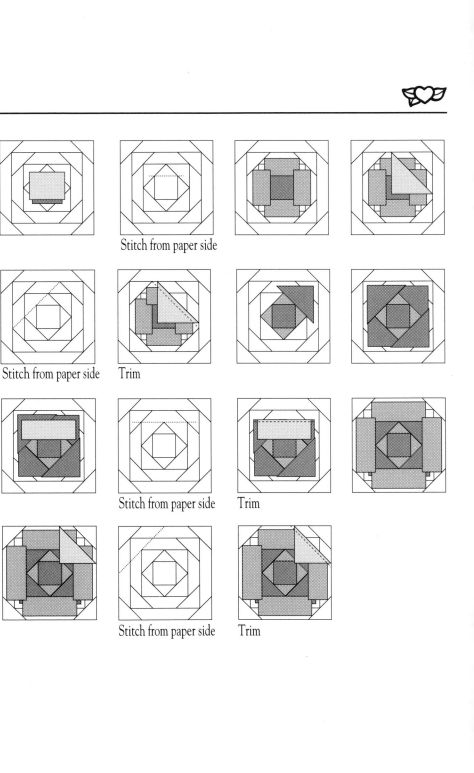

Stitch from paper side

Stitch from paper side   Trim

Stitch from paper side   Trim

Stitch from paper side   Trim

NIGHTTIME MAGIC – 47″ x 47″ – 8½″ block – 9 blocks set 3 x 3

Fancy Free

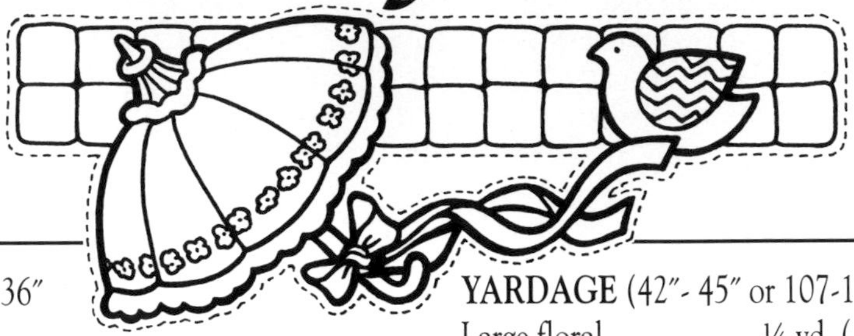

APPROXIMATE SIZE: 36″ x 36″
UNIT SIZE: 1½″
SETTING: Small squares & applique border
TECHNIQUES: Patchwork, applique

YARDAGE (42″- 45″ or 107-114 cm wide):

Large floral	¼ yd. (.3 m)
Very light pink	¼ yd. (.3 m)
Light pink	¼ yd. (.3 m)
Medium pink	¼ yd. (.3 m)
Dark pink	¼ yd. (.3 m)
Very light green	¼ yd. (.3 m)
Light green	¼ yd. (.3 m)
Medium green	¼ yd. (.3 m)
Dark green	¼ yd. (.3 m)
Very dark green	¼ yd. (.3 m)
Border	⅞ yd. (.8 m)
Binding	⅜ yd. (.4 m)
Backing	1¼ yds. (1.2 m)
Batting (packaged)	45″ x 60″
(45″ wide)	1¼ yds. (1.2 m)

CUTTING (Templates on pages 98, 99):
Ar (Br, Cr, etc.) refers to A (B, C, etc.) reversed

Large floral	Template F: 57
Very light pink	Template F: 16
Light pink	Template F: 16
Medium pink	Template F: 32
Dark pink	Template F: 32
Very dark green	Template F: 32
Dark green	Template F: 32
Medium green	Template F: 28
Light green	Template F: 24
Very light green	Template F: 20
Very light pink	Template A, Ar: 3 each
Light pink	Template A, Ar: 3 each
	Template B, C: 2 each
Medium pink	Template A, Ar: 3each
Dark pink	Template A, Ar: 3 each

Continued on page 105

"By sharing with a friend, we are able to see twice the beauty."

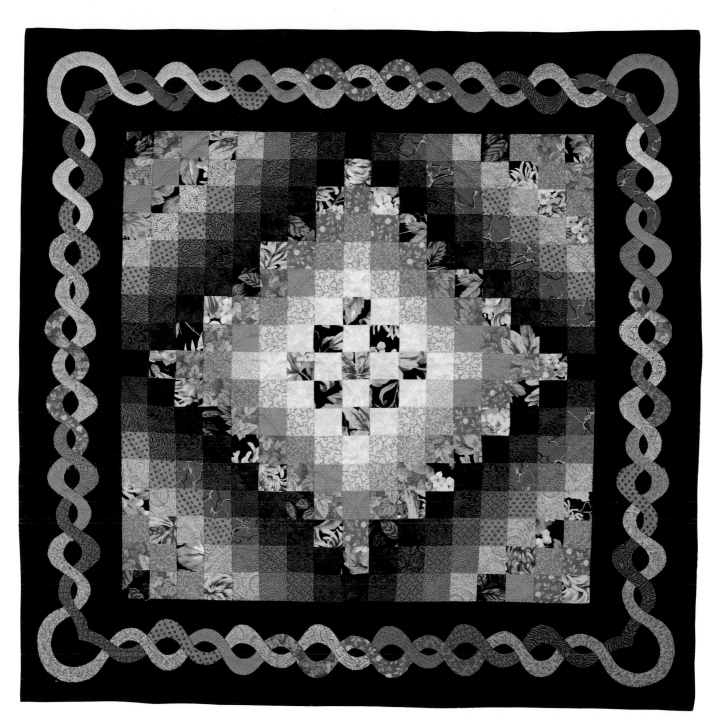

FANCY FREE. 36″ x 36″. Designed, pieced, and quilted by Joyce Stewart, 1991. Applique design from *Quilting Designs from the Amish* by Pepper Cory, C & T Publishing.

FANCY FREE
DIRECTIONS:

Use ¼″ seams throughout. Refer to *General Directions*, page 12, for specific piecing, applique, quilting, and binding directions. Refer to quilt diagram, color photo, and piecing diagrams for order of assembly.

1. Stitch squares (Template F) together in horizontal rows following chart for color placement. Press seams between blocks of even rows to the right and seams between blocks of odd rows to the left. Stitch the rows together and press seams toward bottom of quilt.

2. Add borders, referring to mitered borders section of *General Directions*, page 14.

3. Applique borders. Follow illustrations and color photo for placement of applique. There are two different corner arrangements to applique; corner A appears opposite A, and corner B appears opposite B.

   Note: Turn A 180° - do not flip - as you work along each side that is made up of A. Do the same as you work along each side that is made up of Ar. See diagram. This 180° turn creates the alternating wide "eye" and narrow "eye". Distribute dark, medium, and light A's and Ar's as desired.

4. Refer to *Finishing Steps For All Quilts*, page 12.

5. Quilt center is hand quilted in diagonal lines through corners of small squares; border is quilted next to applique and in diagonal parallel lines ½″ apart.

Wide Eye   Narrow Eye

FANCY FREE – 36″ x 36″ – 1½″ unit – small squares and applique border

1	Large Floral		Very Light Green
2	Very Light Pink		Light Green
3	Light Pink		Medium Green
4	Medium Pink		Dark Green
5	Dark Pink		Very Dark Green

Calico Charm

APPROXIMATE SIZE: 62″ x 62″
BLOCK SIZE: 6″ - 49 blocks set 7 x 7
SETTING: Blocks set straight with narrow sashing
TECHNIQUES: Patchwork, applique

YARDAGE (42″- 45″ or 107-114 cm wide):

Light floral	1¾ yds. (1.6 m)
Dark floral	1¼ yds. (1.2 m)
Pink	2⅝ yds. (2.4 m)
Blue (includes border)	2 yds. (1.9 m)
Binding	⅝ yd. (.6 m)
Backing	3⅞ yds. (3.6 m)
Batting (packaged)	72″ x 90″
(45″ wide)	3¾ yds. (3.5 m)

CUTTING (Templates on pages 99, 100):

Light floral	Template A: 24
	Template B: 128
Pink	Template A: 25
	Template B: 128
	Template G: 28
	Template H: 4
Blue	Template B: 4
	Template C: 28
	Template E: 64
	Border:
	4 lengthwise grain cuts 5″ wide x 66″ long
Dark floral	Template I: 32
	Template J: 32
	Template D: 112
	Template F: 32
Binding	7 crossgrain cuts 2½″ wide

*"To strengthen the heart and make
the spirit sing, reach out and
lift another's soul."*

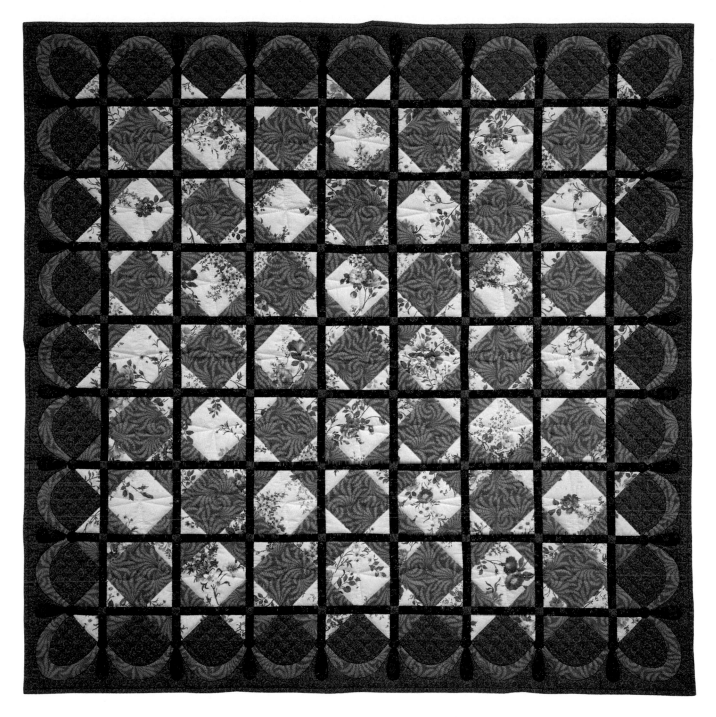

CALICO CHARM. *62″ x 62″. Designed, pieced, and quilted by Joyce Stewart, 1992.*

CALICO CHARM
DIRECTIONS:

Use ¼″ seams throughout. Refer to *General Directions*, page 12, for specific piecing, applique, quilting, and binding directions. Refer to quilt diagram, color photo, and piecing diagrams for order of assembly.

1. Block 1: Make 25 Block 1 with pink centers and light floral corners. Make 24 Block 1 with light floral centers and pink corners.

2. Block 2: Make 12 Block 2 with blue centers and light floral corners. Make 16 Block 2 with blue centers and pink corners.

3. Block 3: Make 4 Block 3 with blue and light floral.

4. Sashing Row: Use Templates D and E to make 8 rows of sashing as illustrated.

5. Block Row: Use Block 1 and Template D to make 4 rows of blocks with pink centers at each end. Use Block 1 and Template D to make 3 rows of blocks with white centers at each end. See illustration.

6. Side Unit Rows: Make 4 rows of Block 2 and Template F with pink-cornered blocks at each end. See illustration.

7. Assemble rows of Block 1 and rows of sashing beginning and ending with sashing rows. Stitch rows of Block 2 to opposite sides of quilt, making sure small triangles face the quilt center. See illustration and color photo. Stitch a Block 3 to each end of the 2 remaining rows of Block 2, making sure white side of Block 3 faces pink triangle across the sashing strip. Stitch these 2 rows of Blocks 2 and 3 to the 2 remaining sides of the quilt, making sure small triangles face the quilt center. See color photo.

8. Add blue borders, refering to mitered borders section of *General Directions*, page 14. Applique the swags, using Templates G, H, I, and J, referring to diagram and color photo for placement.

9. Refer to *Finishing Steps For All Quilts*, page 12.

10. Quilt is hand quilted in the ditch around the edge of piece A and between blocks and sashing. Diagrams and a pattern (page 99) are given for the quilting used in Block 1. The swag border is quilted around each applique piece and in a 1″ crosshatch pattern in the blue sections between the swags and the quilt center.

Block 1 Quilting Guides

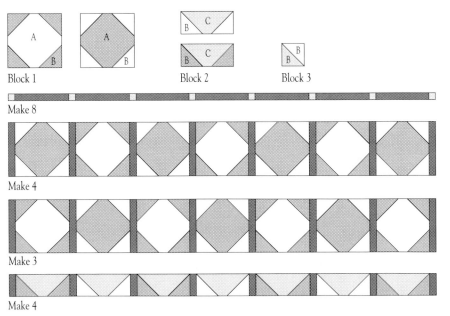

Block 1   Block 2   Block 3

Make 8

Make 4

Make 3

Make 4

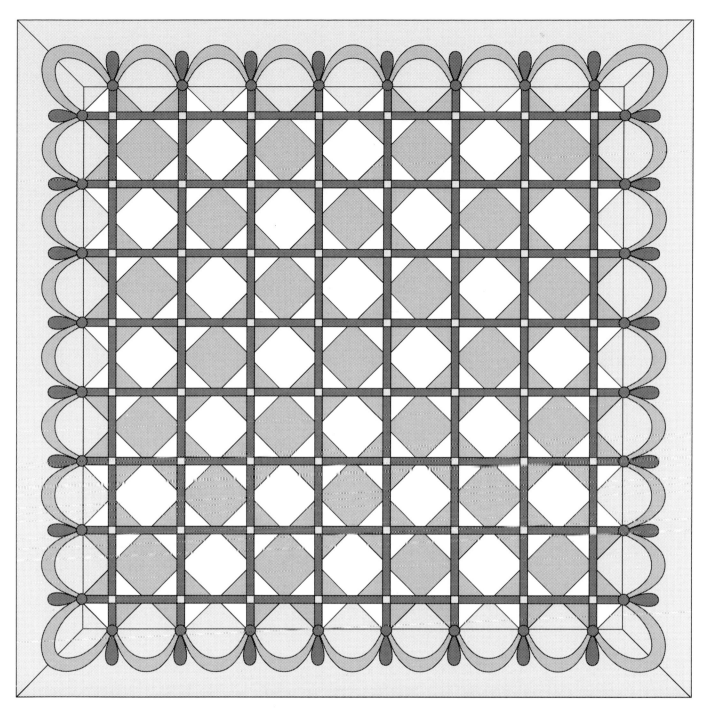

CALICO CHARM – 62″ x 62″ – 6″ block – 49 blocks set 7 x 7

Memories

APPROXIMATE SIZE: 82″ x 102″
BLOCK SIZE: 10″ - 12 blocks set 3 x 4
SETTING: Blocks set on point with frames, finishing triangles, sashing, and applique border
TECHNIQUES: Patchwork, applique

"I've stitched my life into a patchwork quilt. If I am ever lonely, I will wrap my memories around me, and they will keep me warm."

YARDAGE (42″- 45″ or 107-114 cm wide):

Light blue solid (blocks, finishing triangles, border)	5½ yds. (5.1 m)
Dark blue solid (frames)	1 yd. (1 m)
Navy blue print (sashing)	2⅜ yds. (2.2 m)
Dark blue prints (blocks)	to total ⅝ yd. (.6 m)
Medium blue prints (blocks)	to total ⅝ yd. (.6 m)
Light blue print (blocks)	to total ⅝ yd. (.6 m)
Very dark pink (blocks, applique)	to total ⅞ yd. (.8 m)
Medium pink print (blocks)	to total ⅝ yd. (.6 m)
Light pink print (blocks, applique)	1 yd. (1 m)
Green print (stems, leaves)	1½ yds. (1.4 m)
Green prints (blocks, leaves)	to total ½ yd. (.5 m)
Turquoise print (setting squares)	¼ yd. (.3 m)
Binding	1¼ yds. (1.2 m)
Backing	6 yds. (5.5 m)
Batting (packaged)	90″ x 108″
(45″ wide)	6 yds. (5.5 m)
Bias bars	¼″, ½″

CUTTING (Templates on pages 100 - 104):

Ar (Br, Cr, etc.) refers to A (B, C, etc.) reversed

Block 1 - Cross and Crown

Light blue solid	Template A: 4
	Template I: 8
Light blue print	Template A: 1
Medium pink print	Template P: 4
Dark blue print	Template O: 4
Very dark pink	Template I: 8

Block 2 - Pinwheel Square

Light blue solid	Templates B, C, D: 4 each
Light blue print	Template A: 4
Very dark pink	Template B: 4
Medium blue print	Templates C, D: 4 each
Light pink print	Template A: 1

Continued on page 108

Continued on page 108

MEMORIES. *82″ x 102″. Designed, pieced, and quilted by Ann Seely, 1991.*

MEMORIES

DIRECTIONS:

Use ¼″ seams throughout. Refer to *General Directions*, page 12, for specific piecing, applique, quilting, and binding directions. Refer to quilt diagram, color photo, and piecing diagrams for order of assembly.

1. Following diagrams on page 109, make one each of the 12 pieced blocks. Add frames of dark blue solid to each block (Template W). Sample piecing diagrams of horizontal/vertical and diagonal blocks are given on this page.

2. Stitch light blue solid triangles to each block (Template X).

3. Using Templates Y and Z, make 10 setting squares for the sashing.

4. Make 4 rows of blocks with 3 blocks and 2 sashing strips (3½″ x 17½″) in each row. Make 3 rows of sashing with 3 sashing strips and 2 pieced setting squares in each row. Stitch the rows of sashing and the rows of blocks together beginning and ending with rows of blocks.

5. Sew the 3½″ x 77½″ sashing strips to the sides of the quilt. Sew pieced setting squares to each end of the 57½″ sashing strips and then sew them to the top and bottom of the quilt.

6. Add borders. Refer to mitered border section of *General Directions*, page 14.

7. Applique the borders. Evenly space the 80″ curving vines along the top and bottom borders and the 105″ curving vines along the side borders. Tulip is made from 3 overlapping piece DD. Leaf is AA. Refer to quilt diagram and color photo for placement of stems, flowers, and leaves.

8. Refer to *Finishing Steps For All Quilts*, page 12. Use a ⅝″ seam allowance to attach binding.

9. Quilt is ditch quilted by hand in the blocks and around the frames. A bow is quilted in each finishing triangle

around the blocks (pattern on page 104). A rope is quilted in the sashing (pattern on page 104). The border is crosshatch quilted in 1⅛″ squares on the diagonal and around all appliques.

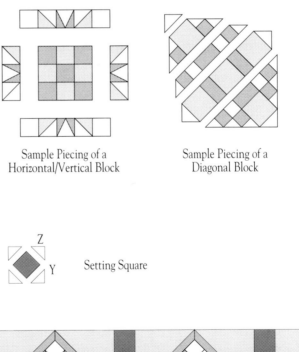

Sample Piecing of a
Horizontal/Vertical Block

Sample Piecing of a
Diagonal Block

Setting Square

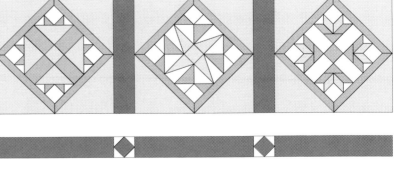

MEMORIES – 82″ x 102″ – 10″ block – 12 blocks set 3 x 4

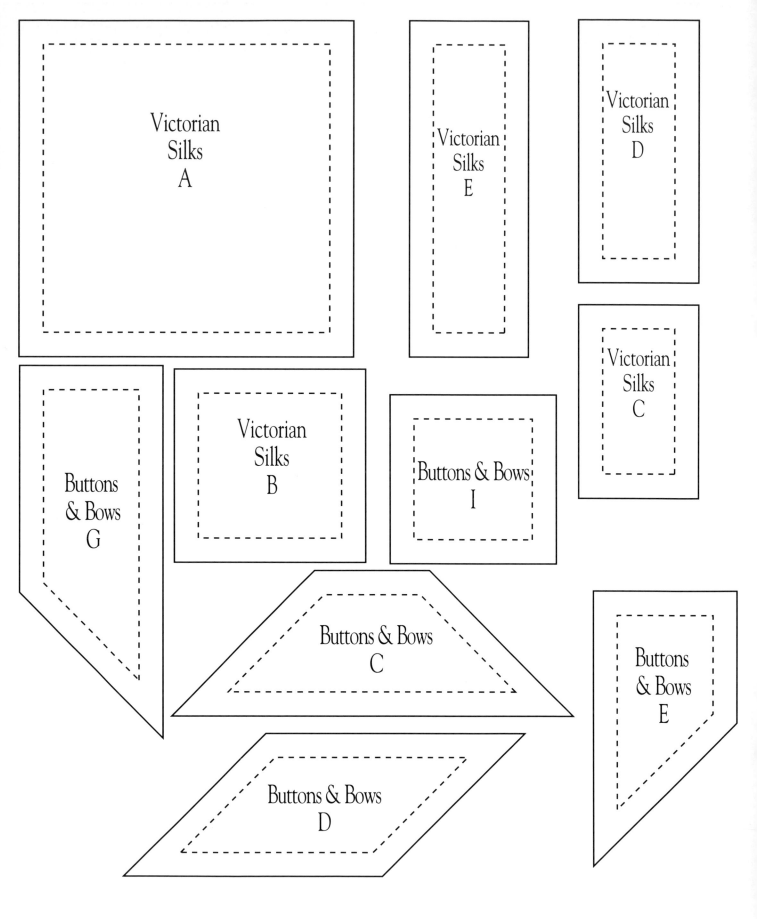

Victorian
Silks
A

Victorian
Silks
E

Victorian
Silks
D

Victorian
Silks
C

Victorian
Silks
B

Buttons
& Bows
G

Buttons & Bows
I

Buttons & Bows
C

Buttons
& Bows
E

Buttons & Bows
D

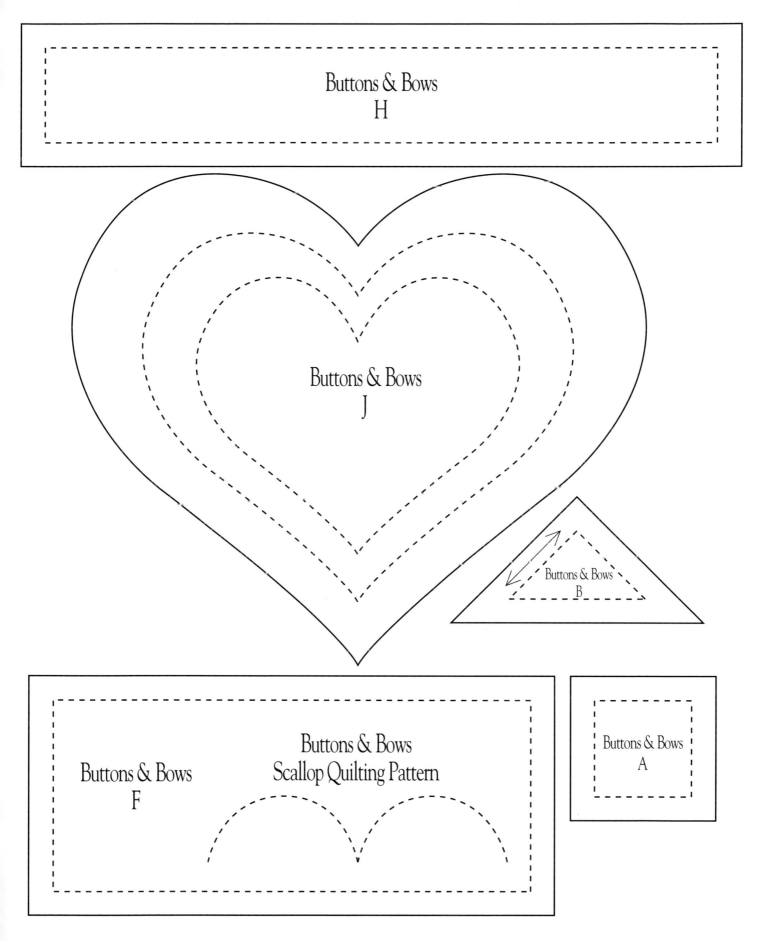

Buttons & Bows
H

Buttons & Bows
J

Buttons & Bows
B

Buttons & Bows
Scallop Quilting Pattern

Buttons & Bows
F

Buttons & Bows
A

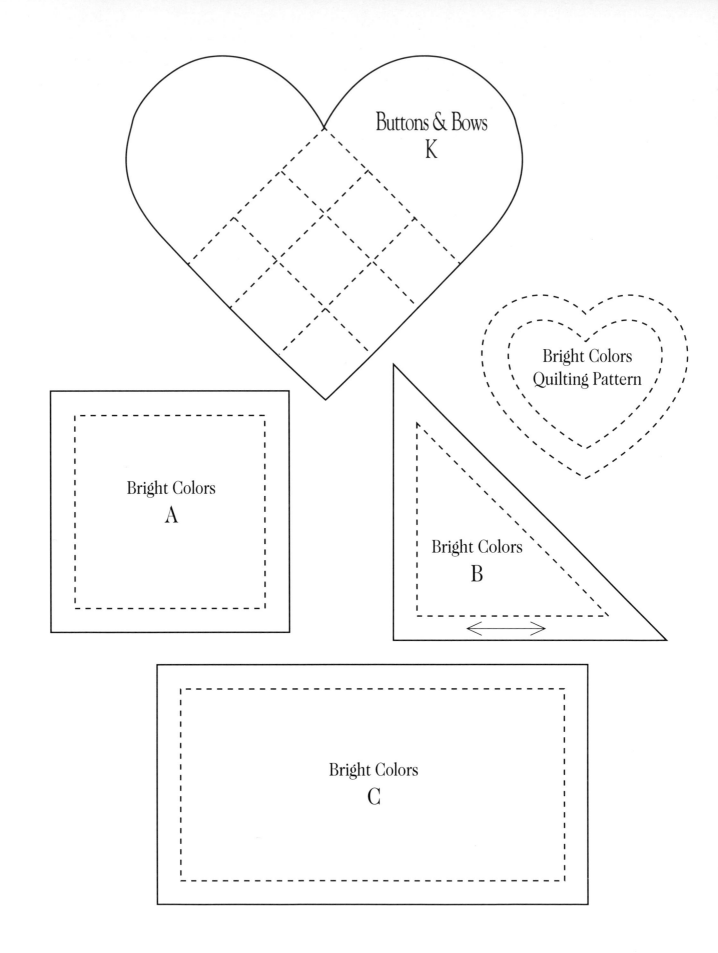

Buttons & Bows
K

Bright Colors
Quilting Pattern

Bright Colors
A

Bright Colors
B

Bright Colors
C

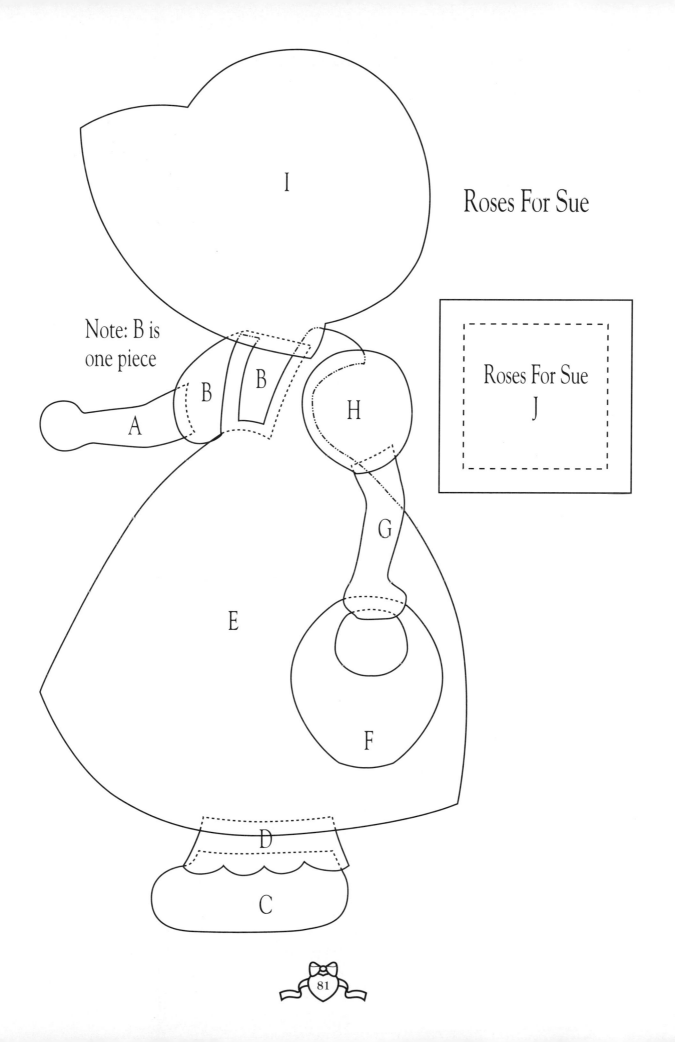

Roses For Sue

Note: B is one piece

Roses For Sue
J

81

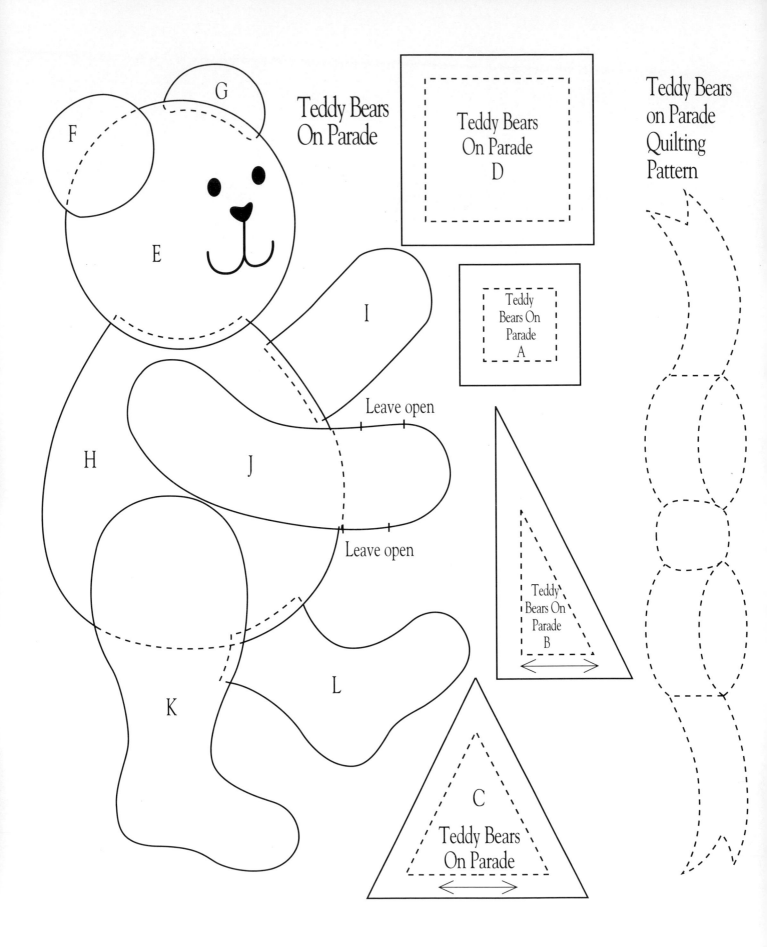

Teddy Bears
On Parade

Teddy Bears
On Parade
D

Teddy Bears
on Parade
Quilting
Pattern

Teddy
Bears On
Parade
A

Leave open

Leave open

Teddy
Bears On
Parade
B

C
Teddy Bears
On Parade

G

F

E

I

H

J

K

L

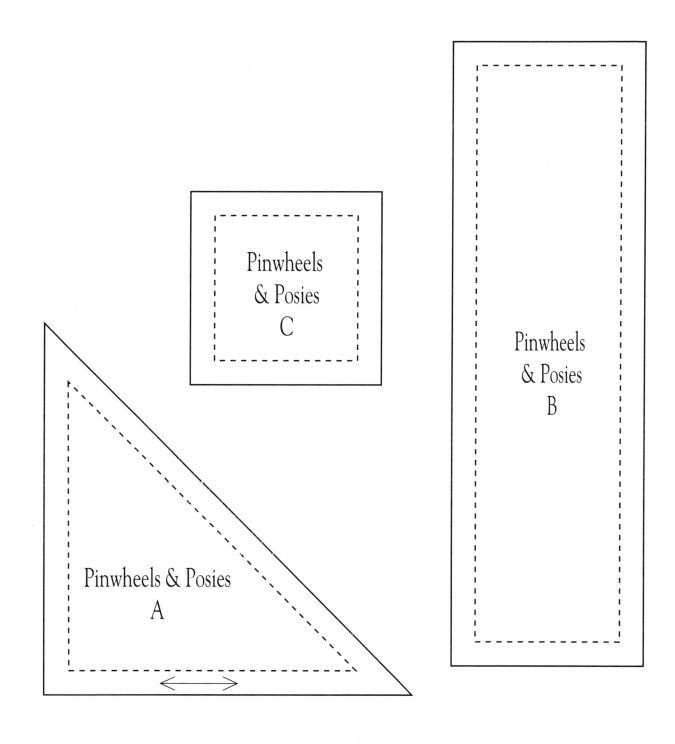

Pinwheels
& Posies
C

Pinwheels
& Posies
B

Pinwheels & Posies
A

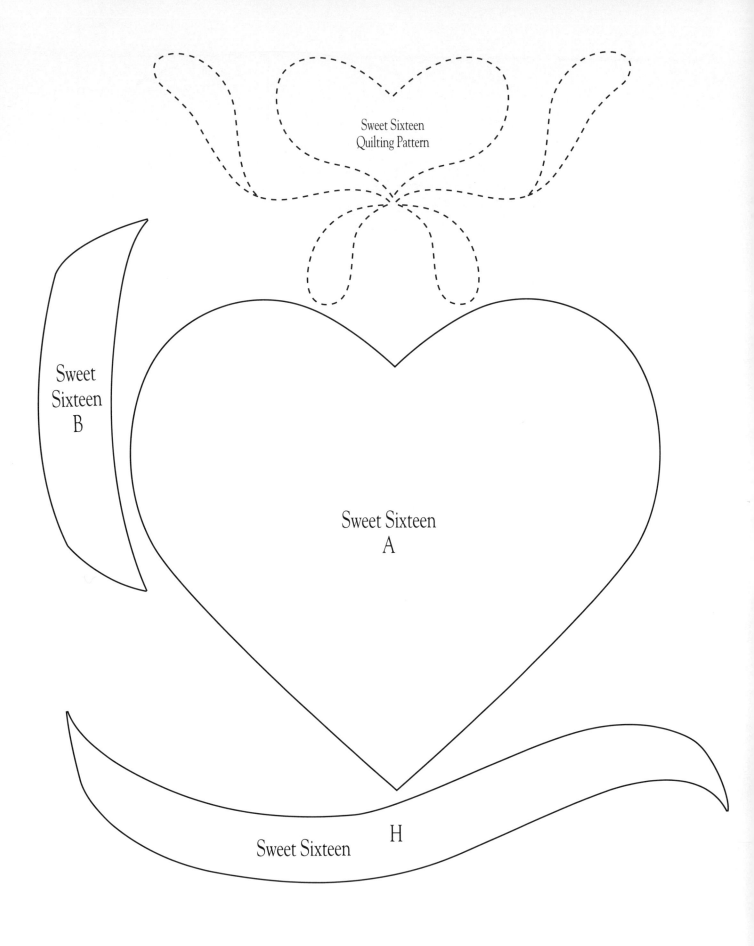

Sweet Sixteen
Quilting Pattern

Sweet
Sixteen
B

Sweet Sixteen
A

Sweet Sixteen H

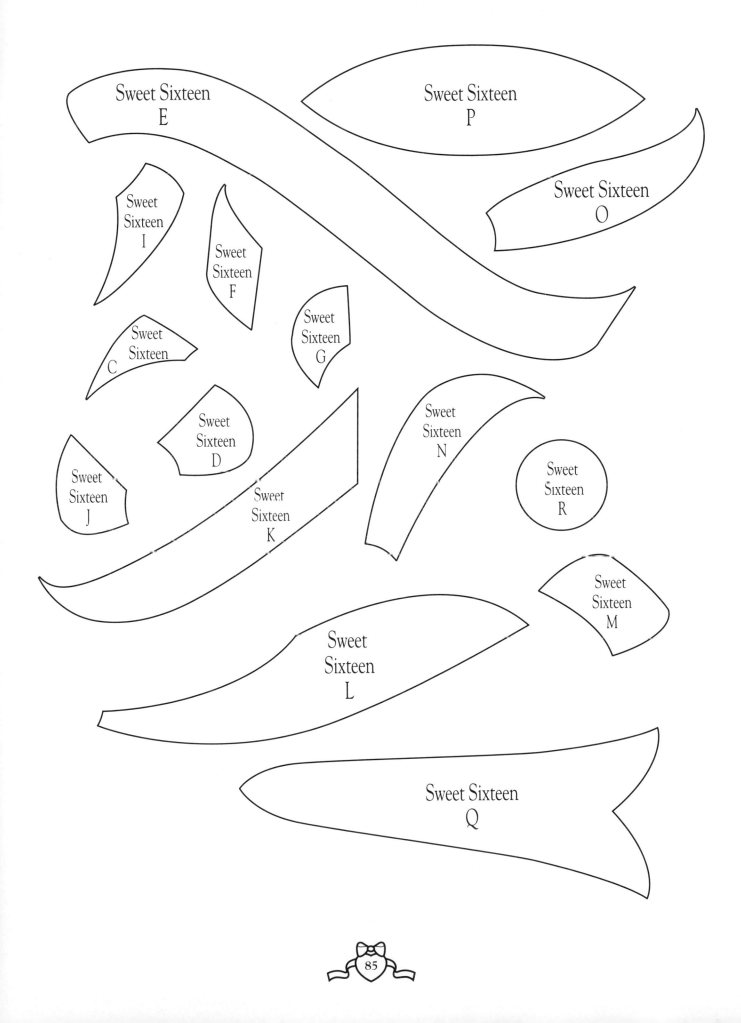

Sweet Sixteen
E

Sweet Sixteen
P

Sweet Sixteen
O

Sweet
Sixteen
I

Sweet
Sixteen
F

Sweet
Sixteen
C

Sweet
Sixteen
G

Sweet
Sixteen
D

Sweet
Sixteen
N

Sweet
Sixteen
R

Sweet
Sixteen
J

Sweet
Sixteen
K

Sweet
Sixteen
M

Sweet
Sixteen
L

Sweet Sixteen
Q

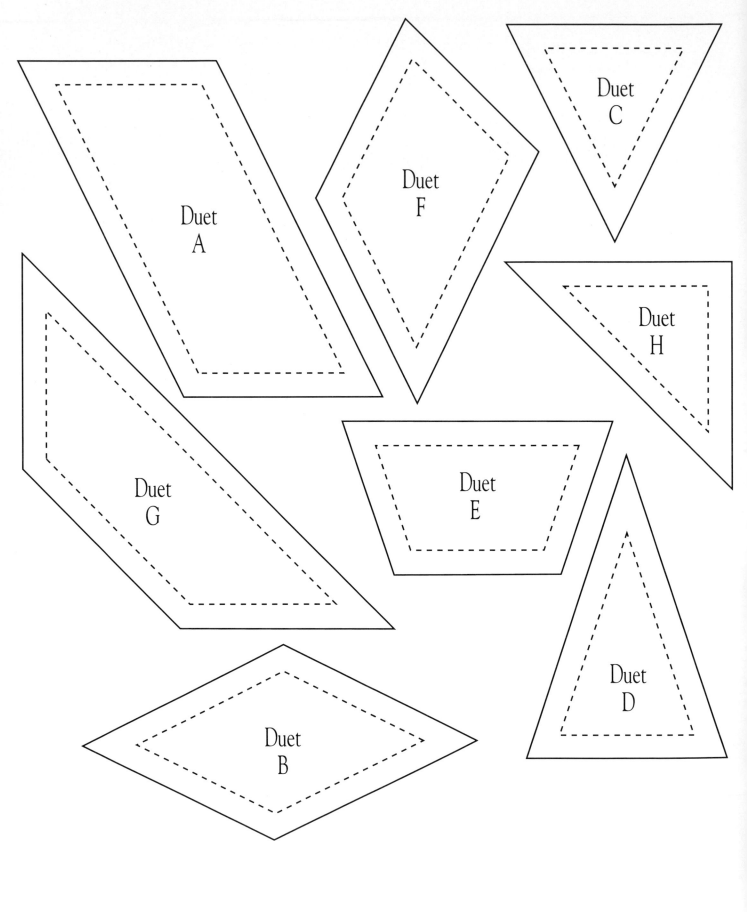

Duet
A

Duet
F

Duet
C

Duet
H

Duet
G

Duet
E

Duet
D

Duet
B

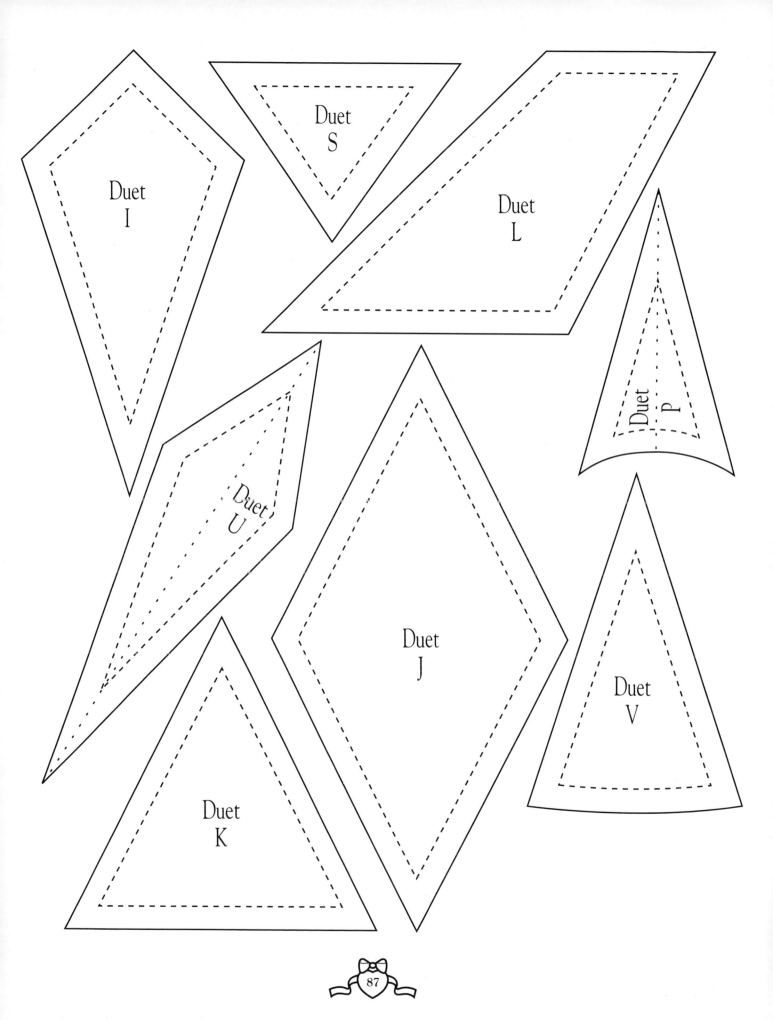

Duet
I

Duet
S

Duet
L

Duet
P

Duet
U

Duet
J

Duet
V

Duet
K

87

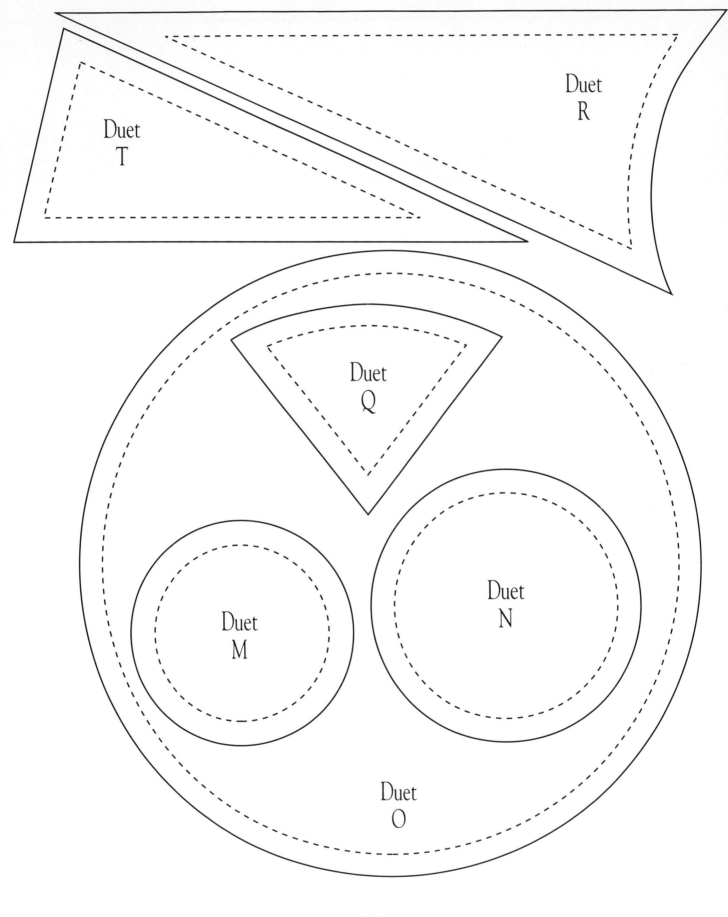

Duet
R

Duet
T

Duet
Q

Duet
N

Duet
M

Duet
O

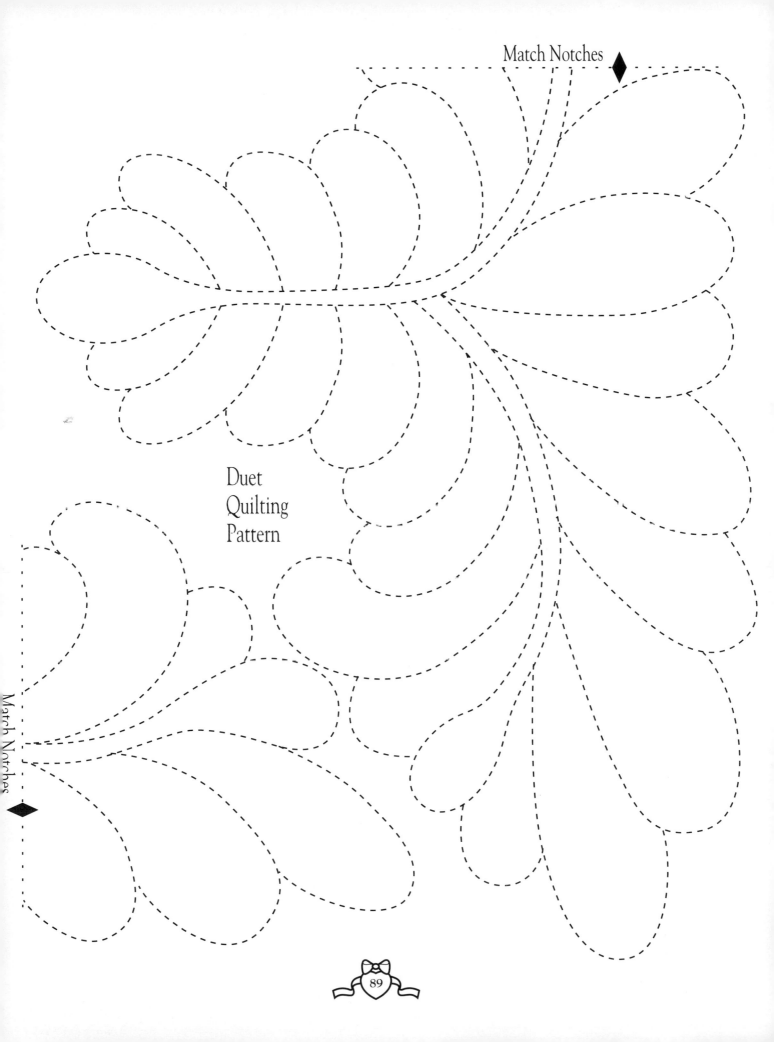

Match Notches

Duet
Quilting
Pattern

Match Notches

89

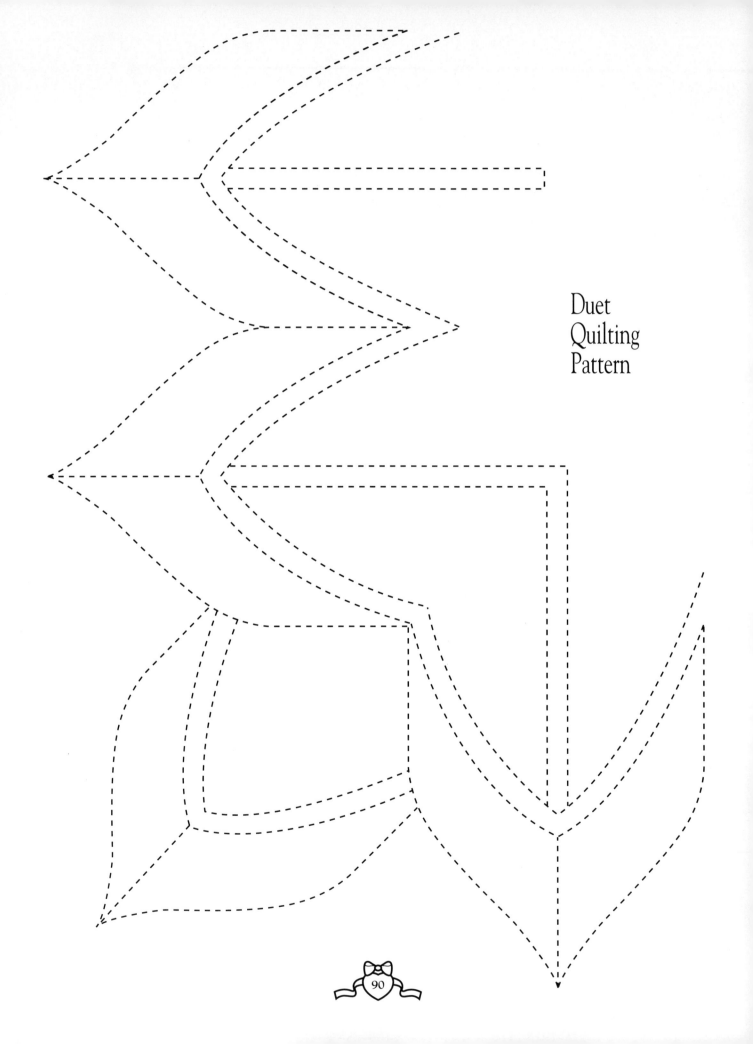

Duet
Quilting
Pattern

90

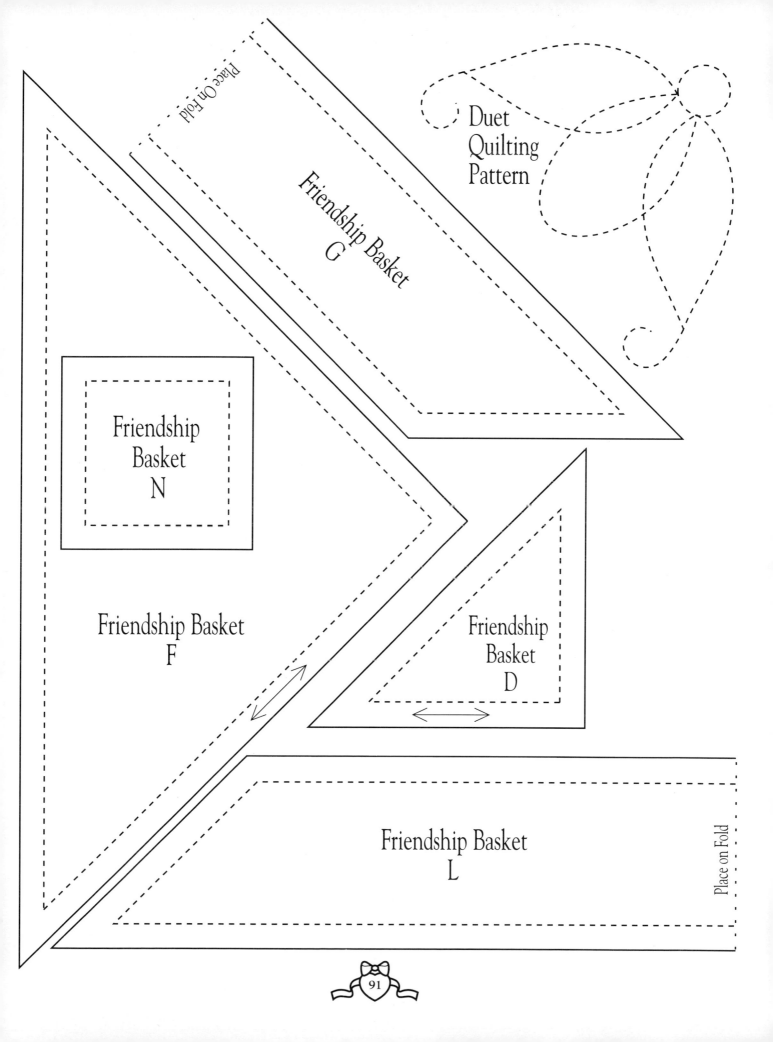

Duet
Quilting
Pattern

Friendship Basket
G

Place On Fold

Friendship
Basket
N

Friendship Basket
F

Friendship
Basket
D

Friendship Basket
L

Place on Fold

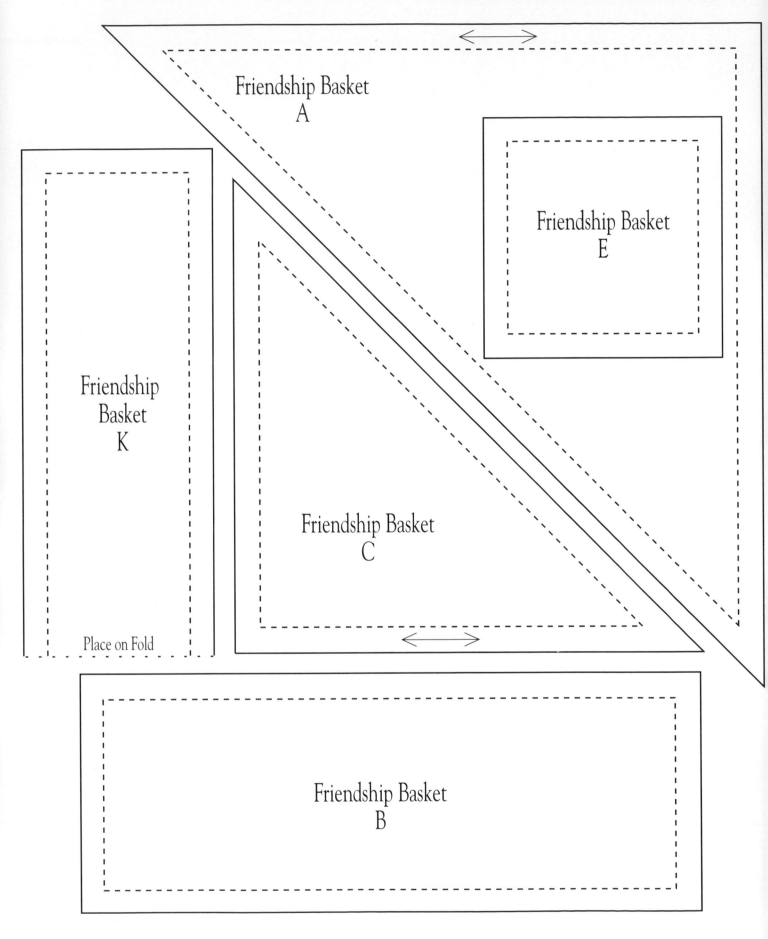

Friendship Basket
A

Friendship Basket
E

Friendship
Basket
K

Place on Fold

Friendship Basket
C

Friendship Basket
B

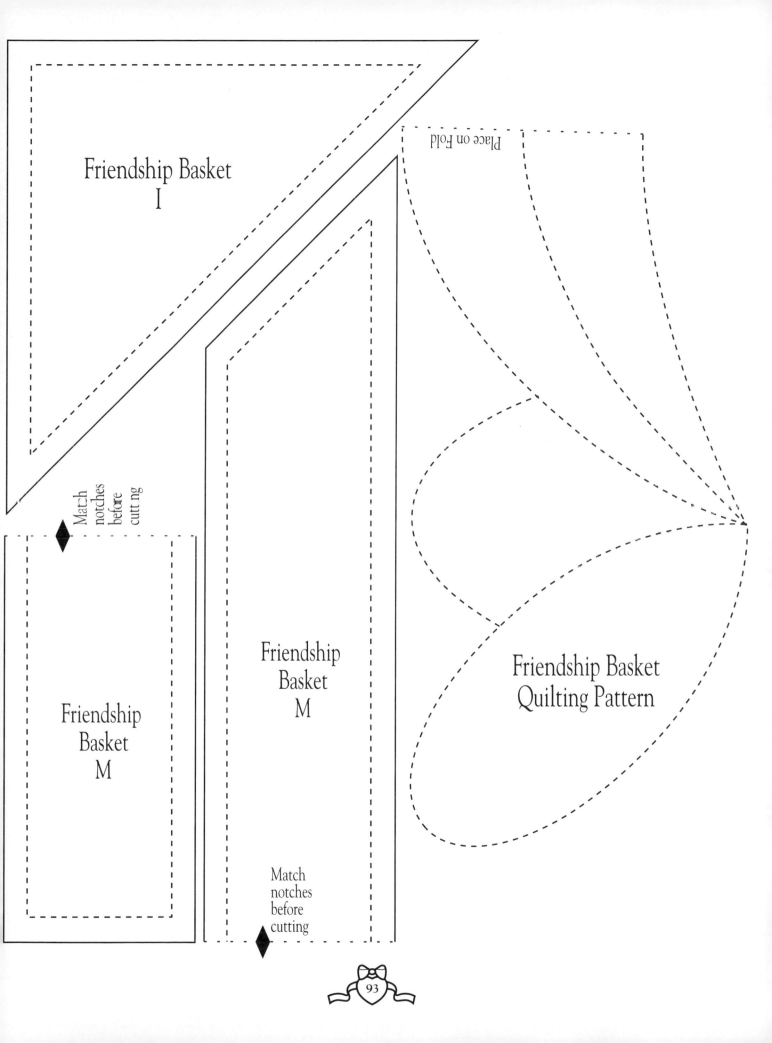

Friendship Basket
I

Friendship Basket
M

Friendship
Basket
M

Match
notches
before
cutting

Match
notches
before
cutting

Place on Fold

Friendship Basket
Quilting Pattern

93

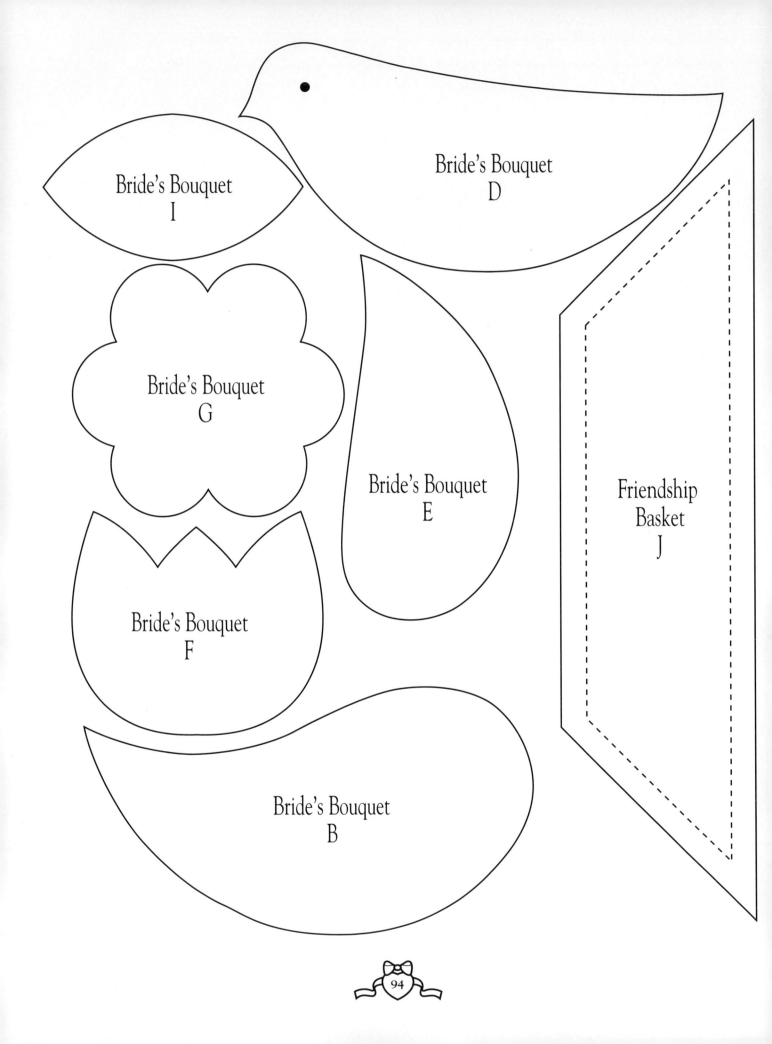

Bride's Bouquet
I

Bride's Bouquet
D

Bride's Bouquet
G

Bride's Bouquet
E

Friendship
Basket
J

Bride's Bouquet
F

Bride's Bouquet
B

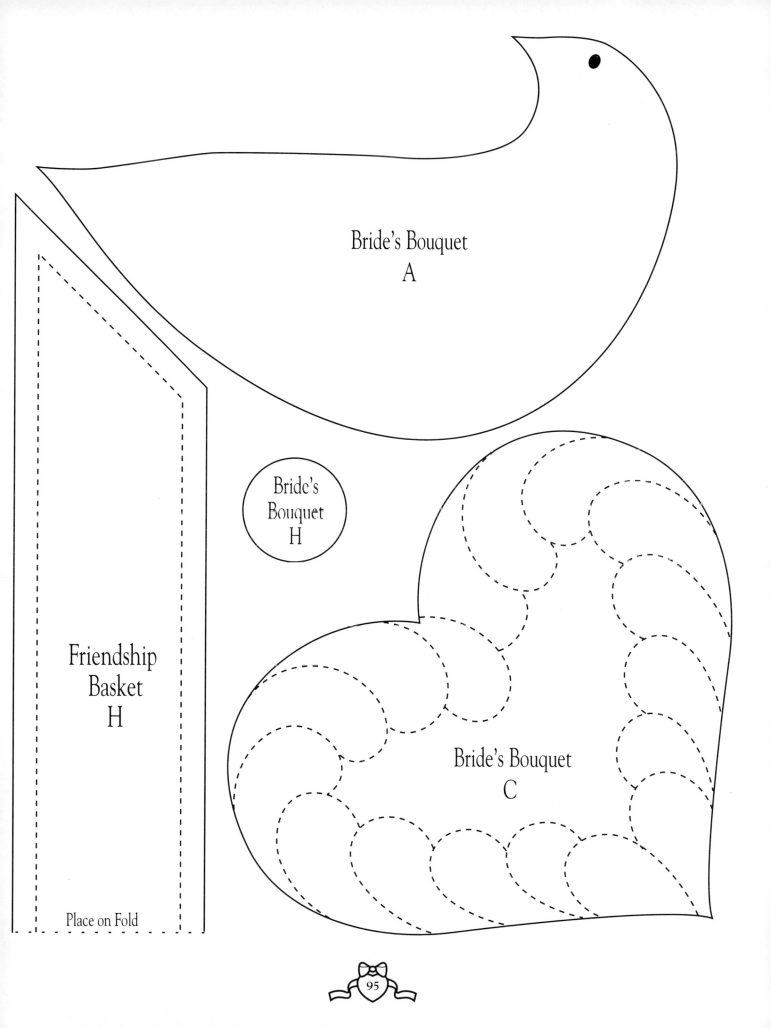

Bride's Bouquet
A

Bride's
Bouquet
H

Friendship
Basket
H

Bride's Bouquet
C

Place on Fold

95

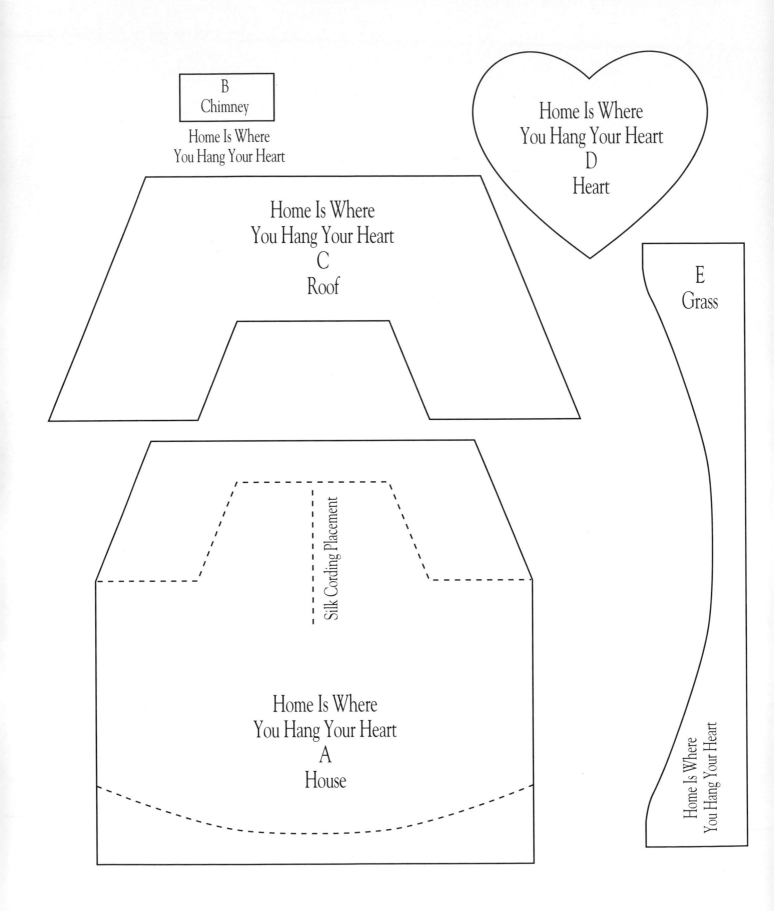

B
Chimney

Home Is Where
You Hang Your Heart

Home Is Where
You Hang Your Heart
C
Roof

Home Is Where
You Hang Your Heart
D
Heart

E
Grass

Silk Cording Placement

Home Is Where
You Hang Your Heart
A
House

Home Is Where
You Hang Your Heart

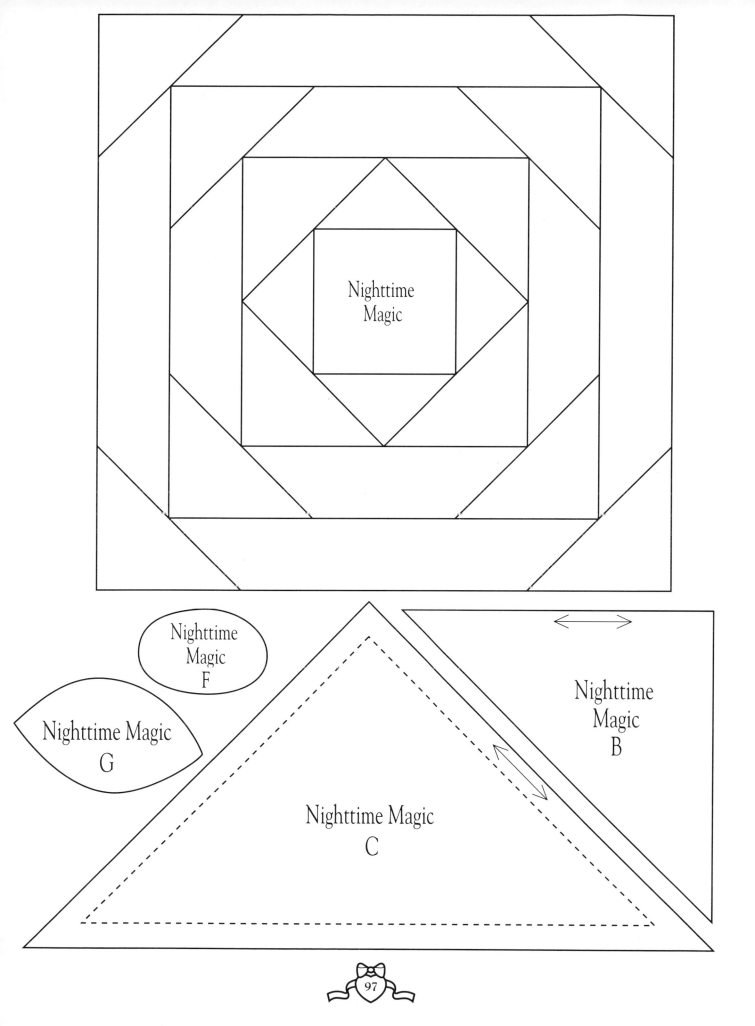

Nighttime
Magic

Nighttime
Magic
F

Nighttime Magic
G

Nighttime Magic
C

Nighttime
Magic
B

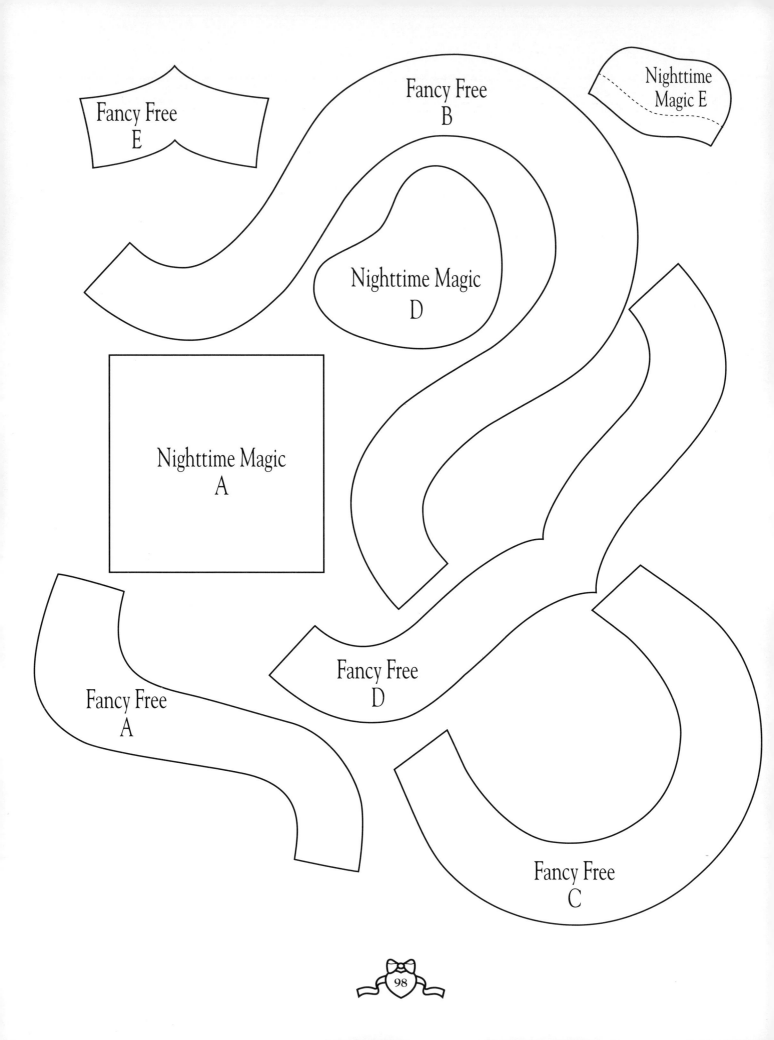

Fancy Free
E

Fancy Free
B

Nighttime
Magic E

Nighttime Magic
D

Nighttime Magic
A

Fancy Free
D

Fancy Free
A

Fancy Free
C

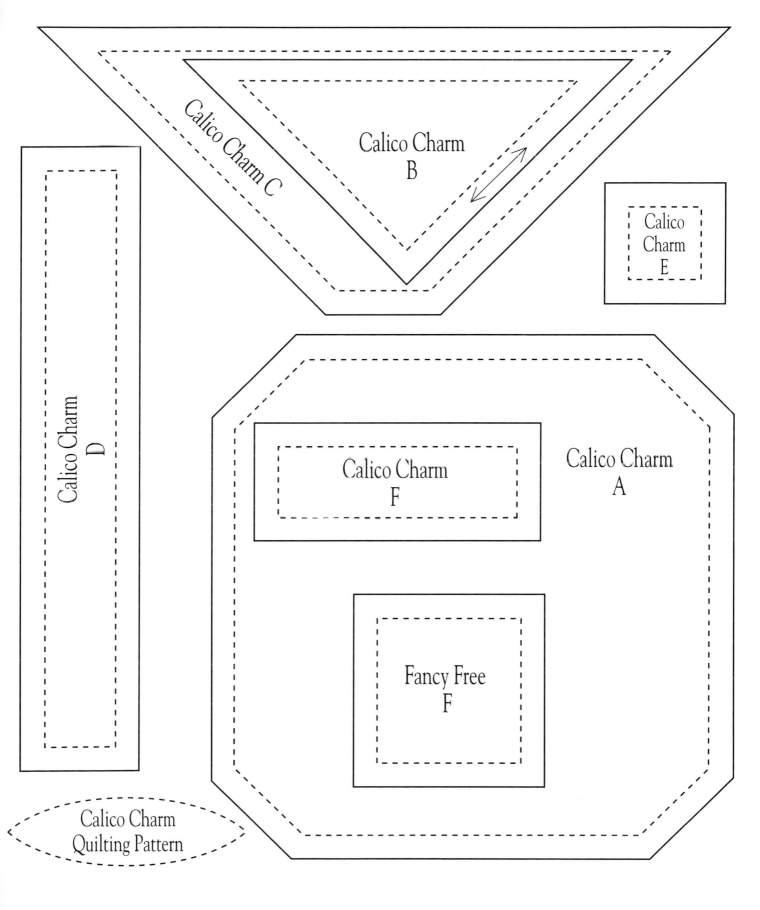

Calico Charm C

Calico Charm
B

Calico
Charm
E

Calico Charm
D

Calico Charm
A

Calico Charm
F

Fancy Free
F

Calico Charm
Quilting Pattern

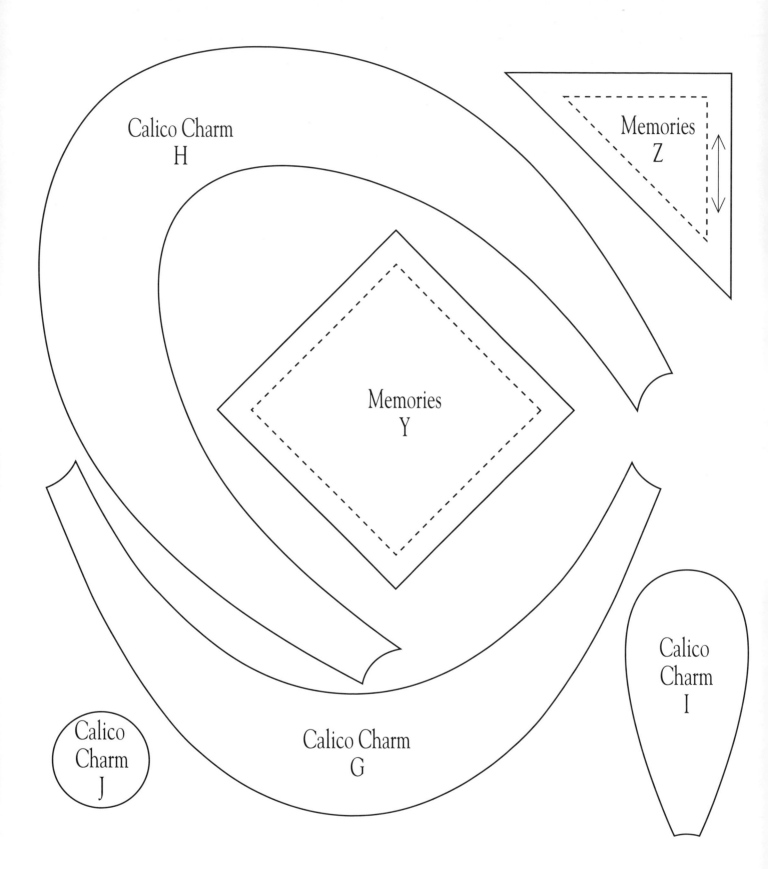

Calico Charm
H

Memories
Z

Memories
Y

Calico
Charm
J

Calico Charm
G

Calico
Charm
I

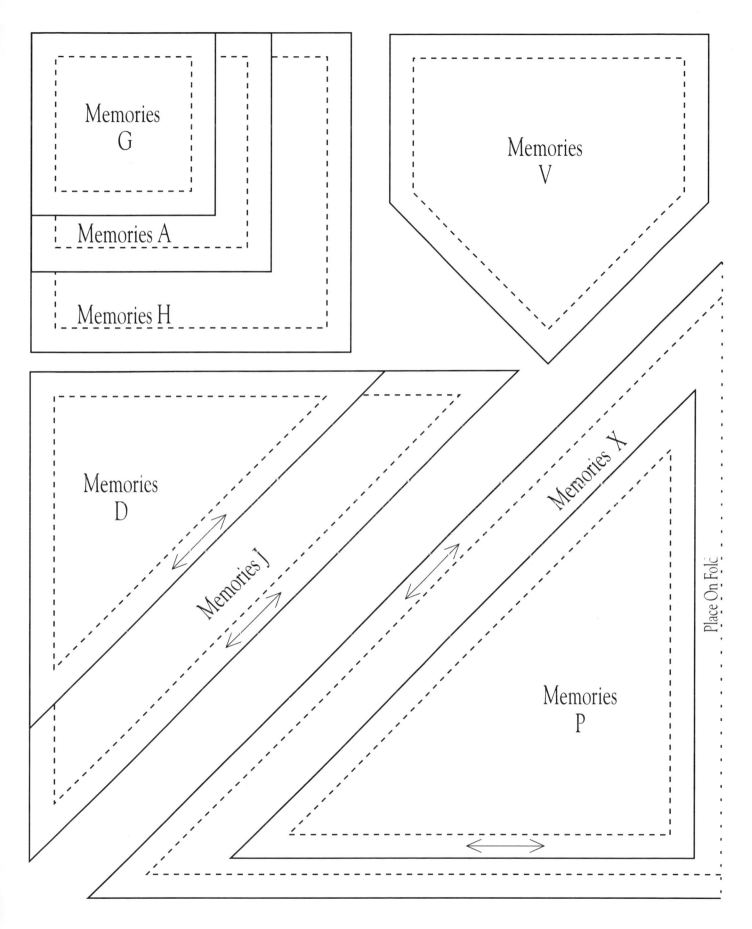

Memories
G

Memories A

Memories H

Memories
V

Memories
D

Memories J

Memories X

Place On Fold

Memories
P

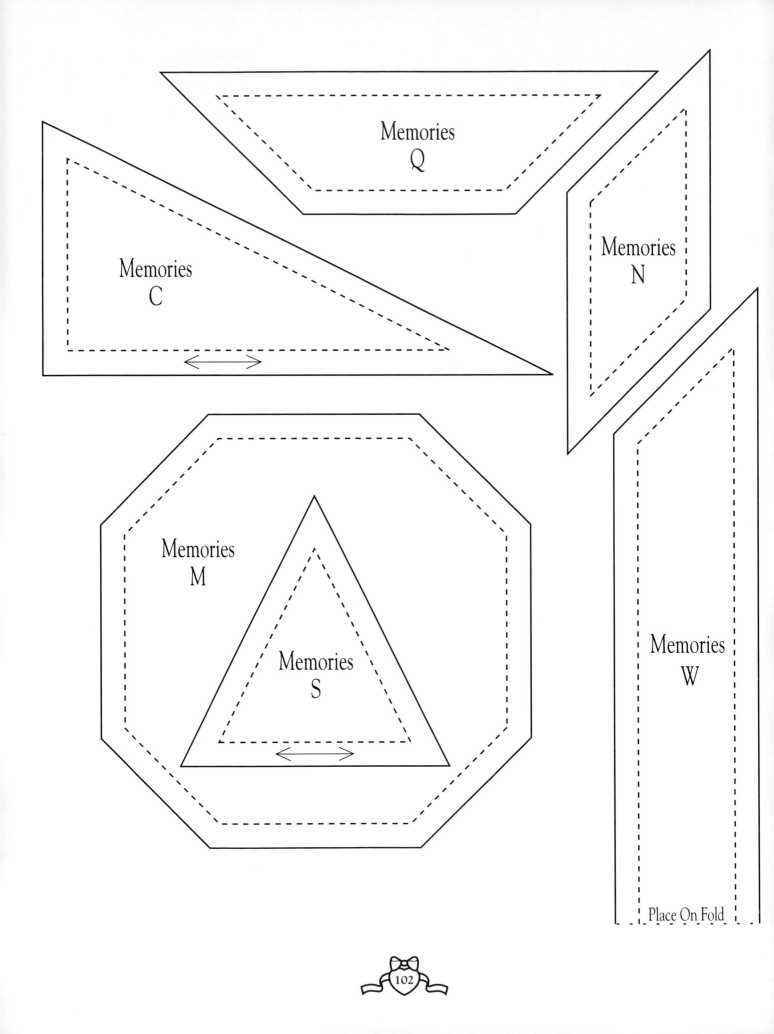

Memories
Q

Memories
C

Memories
N

Memories
M

Memories
S

Memories
W

Place On Fold

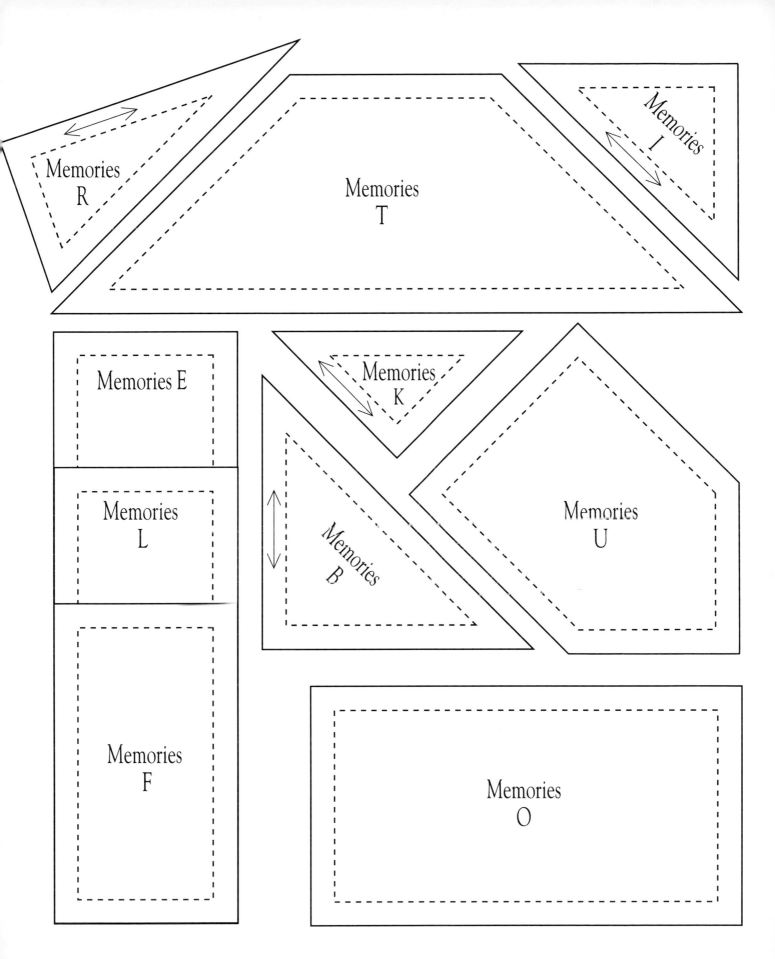

Memories
R

Memories
T

Memories
I

Memories E

Memories
K

Memories
L

Memories
B

Memories
U

Memories
F

Memories
O

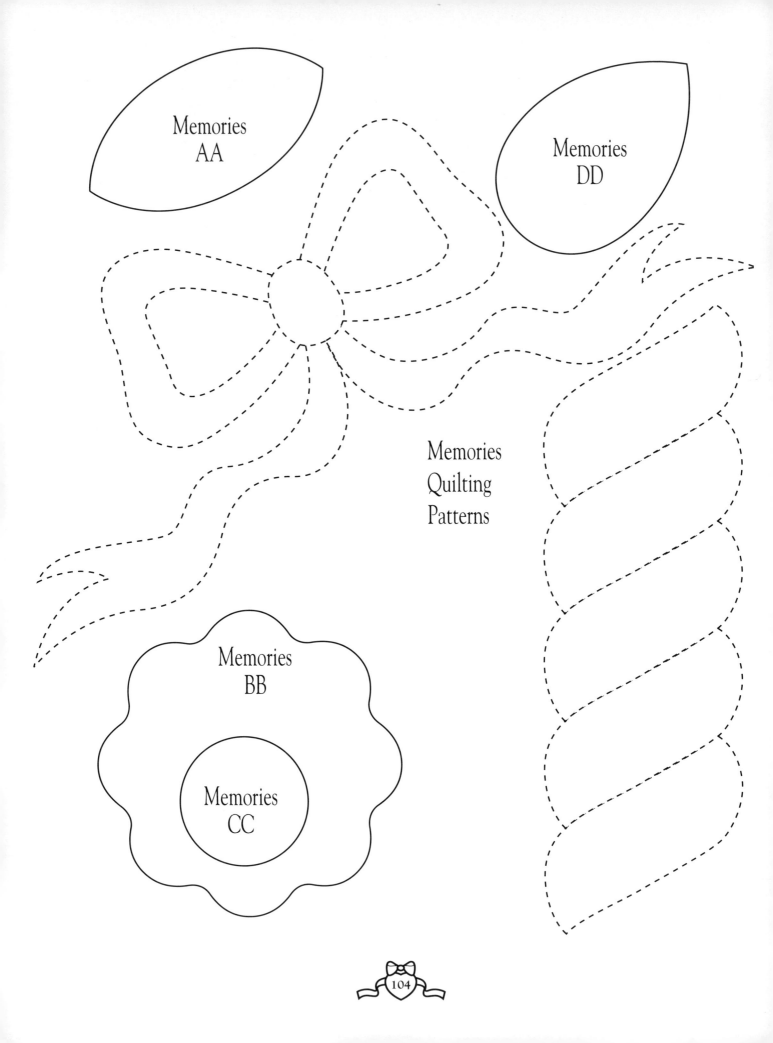

Memories
AA

Memories
DD

Memories
Quilting
Patterns

Memories
BB

Memories
CC

BUTTONS AND BOWS

Continued from page 22

White (continued)	7½" x 7½" (cut 4)
	Border 1: 2¼" x 25½" (cut 2)
	Border 1: 2¼" x 29" (cut 2)
Dark blue	Border 2: 1¾" x 29" (cut 2)
	Border 2: 1¾" x 31½" (cut 2)
	Border 4: 2½" x 45½" (cut 2)
	Border 4: 2½" x 49½" (cut 2)
Light blue	Template J: 4
Assorted pastels	Template I: 144
	Template K: 4
	5½" x 5½" (cut 16)
Binding	5 crossgrain cuts 2½" wide

ROSES FOR SUE

Continued from page 30

Basket	Template F: 9
Hat	Template I: 9
Sashing:	
Large floral	1½" x 9" (cut 12)
	1½" x 11" (cut 12)
Black	¾" x 9" (cut 24)
	¾" x 11" (cut 24)
	Template J: 16
Border:	
Cream	Template J: 66
Medium floral	Template J: 108
Dark pink	Template J: 104
Medium pink	Template J: 38
Dark green	Template J: 78
Medium green	Template J: 38
Binding	5 crossgrain cuts 2½" wide

BRIDE'S BOUQUET

Continued from page 54

Green	Template I: 22
Bouquet stems	1¼" x 11" bias strips (cut 4)
Lower stems	1¾" x 9" bias strips (cut 2)
Upper stems	1½" x 14" bias strips (cut 2)
Light blue solid	Templates D, Dr, F: 1 each
Light blue print	Templates E, Er: 1 each
Medium blue solid	Templates A, Ar: 1 each
Medium blue print	Templates B, Br: 1 each
Medium pink solid	Template C: 1
Dark pink print	Template G: 2
Light yellow	Template G: 2
Yellow print	Template H: 2
Orange	Template F: 2
Light pink solid	Template G: 4
	Template H: 2
Light pink print	Template H: 2
Dark pink solid	Templates F, H: 1 each
Medium pink print	Template G: 1
Binding	3 crossgrain cuts 2½" wide

FANCY FREE

Continued from page 66

Medium green	Templates A, Ar: 4 each
	Templates D, E: 2 each
Light green	Template A, Ar: 4 each
Very light green	Template A, Ar: 4 each
Border	4 crossgrain cuts 6" wide
Binding	4 crossgrain cuts 2½" wide

Continued from page 46

Gray	Template N: 1	Medium turquoise	Template B: 40
	Template O: 1		Template E: 2
			Template F: 2
Black & gray			Template Fr: 2
(see **DIRECTIONS** before cutting)	Template P: 8	Light pink border	4 lengthwise grain cuts
Light pink	Template Q: 8		5¾" x 52"
Dark green	Template R: 8		
Black floral	Template T: 8	Pieced Block Border:	
Tan	Template S: 8	Gray	6 crossgrain cuts 1½"
Dark & light turquoise			wide pieced into four
(see **DIRECTIONS** before cutting)	Template U: 16		54" lengths
Light pink	Template V: 32		8 crossgrain cuts 1½"
	17¾" x 17¾" (cut 1)		wide pieced into four
	16⅝" x 16⅝" (cut 2)		74" lengths
Narrow turquoise stripe	2¼" x 23" (cut 4)	Dark green	Template I: 96
Ribbon Border:		Cream	Template J: 96
Dark pink	1½" x 32" (cut 4)	Turquoise	Template K: 192
	Template C: 40	Pink print	Template L: 96
	Template D: 4		Template Lr: 96
Light pink	Template C: 44	Outside border	4 lengthwise grain cuts
	Template H: 4		9¾" x 95"
Dark turquoise	Template A: 22	Binding	10 crossgrain cuts
	Template Ar: 22		2½" wide
	Template G: 2		

Make 2

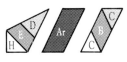

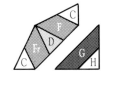

Make 2

Cutting Continued from page 62

Strips for Magic Blocks

Greens - darks	1½" x 2¾" (cut 4)	
mediums	1½" x 4" (cut 4)	
lights	1¾" x 5½" (cut 4)	
Pinks - darks	1½" x 2¾" (cut 12)	
mediums	1½" x 4" (cut 12)	
lights	1¾" x 5½" (cut 12)	
Blues - lights	1½" x 2¾" (cut 20)	
mediums	1½" x 4" (cut 20)	
darks	1¾" x 5½" (cut 20)	
Binding	5 crossgrain cuts 2½" wide	

Directions Continued from page 64

e. Place B on diagonal line, right sides together with long edge of B lined up approximately ⅜" from seamline underneath. See illustration. Stitch from paper side. Turn block over and trim seam to ¼". Flip B over and press. Repeat for other 3 dark triangular corners.

f. Stitch 1½" x 4" strips to this new square, following the method explained in steps c and d. Trim seams to ¼"; flip strips over and press.

g. Repeat step e for second row of dark corners.

h. Repeat step f using 1¾" x 5½" strips for the 3rd light row.

i. Repeat step g for 3rd row of dark corners; begin and end stitching ½" beyond seamline.

j. From paper side, trim block to 6½", ¼" **outside** pencil line indicating 6" block. Remove paper.

2. Stitch C triangles to each side of each Magic Block to make 8½" blocks: Pink block gets light pink triangles; blue blocks get dark blue triangles; three-color blocks get light pink triangles on the pink sides, light green triangles on the green sides, and dark blue triangles on the blue sides.

3. Sew the 9 blocks together in 3 rows of 3 blocks each, referring to photo for color placement.

4. Make 20 units of navy and light green triangles (C). Make 8 units of navy and light pink triangles (C).

5. Make top and bottom rows following diagram. Sew to the top and bottom of the quilt, making sure pink triangles are next to quilt center. Make side rows following diagram and sew to the sides of the quilt, making sure that the pink triangles are always next to the quilt center. See photo.

6. Add navy borders, referring to mitered borders section of *General Directions*, page 14.

7. Applique the floral border in this order: short stems, long stems, all Template E, all Template D, all Template F, all Template G.

8. Refer to *Finishing Steps For All Quilts*, page 12.

9. Quilt is hand quilted in the ditch in the pineapple blocks, ¼" from seams in the triangles, close to appliques, and in a 1" diagonal crosshatch pattern in the border.

Make 2 for Top & Bottom

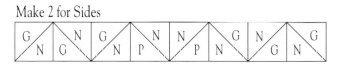

G = Green
N = Navy
P = Pink

Make 2 for Sides

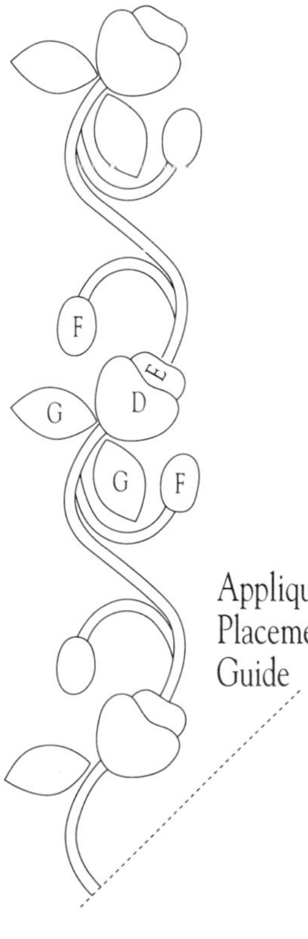

Applique Placement Guide

Continued from page 74

Block 3 - Flying Darts

Light blue solid	Template A: 4
	Template I: 8
Green print	Template B: 4
Very dark pink	Templates N, Nr: 4 each
Light pink print	Templates N, Nr: 4 each
Dark blue print	Template A: 1
Light blue print	Template O: 4

Block 4 - Godey Design

Light blue solid	Template B: 4
	Template I: 24
Light blue print	Template J: 4
Medium blue print	Template B: 8
Medium pink print	Template B: 4
Green print	Template H: 1

Block 5 - King David's Crown

Light blue solid	Templates A, I: 4 each
	Template B: 8
Very dark pink	Template B: 8
Light pink print	Templates B, I: 4 each
Medium blue print	Template I: 8
Dark blue print	Template Q: 4
Medium pink print	Template D: 4

Block 6 - All Kinds

Light blue solid	Template I: 8
Light blue print	Template D: 8
	Template K: 4
Dark blue print	Templates D, L: 4 each
Very dark pink	Template I: 4
Light pink print	Template M: 1

Block 7 - Providence

Light blue solid	Template A: 4
	Template B: 8
Light blue print	Template I: 4
Very dark pink	Template A: 1
Medium pink print	Template V: 4
Dark blue print	Template U: 4
Medium blue print	Template B: 8

Block 8 - Square and a Half

Light blue solid	Template B: 12
Very dark pink	Template B: 4
	Template I: 8
Medium pink print	Template A: 4
Light pink print	Template I: 8
Medium blue print	Template T: 4
Dark blue print	Template A: 1

Block 9 - Album

Light blue solid	Templates B, G: 4 each
	Template I: 12
Dark blue print	Template E: 4
Green print	Template F: 8
Very dark pink	Template H: 1

Block 10 - Triangle Puzzle

Light blue solid	Templates A, S: 4 each
	Template B: 8
Green print	Template B: 8
Dark blue print	Templates R, Rr: 4 each
Medium blue print	Template A: 5
Light pink print	Template A: 4

Block 11 - Goose Tracks

Light blue solid	Templates A, I: 8 each
Very dark pink	Templates N, Nr: 4 each
Dark blue print	Templates N, Nr: 4 each
Medium blue print	Template A: 4
Light pink print	Template A: 1
	Template B: 4

Block 12 - Domino Square

Light blue solid	Template B: 4
	Template I: 12
Light blue print	Templates G, H: 4 each
Very dark pink	Template G: 8
Dark blue print	Template F: 4
Medium pink print	Template H: 1

Frames

Dark blue solid	Template W: 48

Finishing triangles

Light blue solid	Template X: 48

Sashing

Navy blue print	Template Y: 10
	3½″ x 17½″ (cut 17)
	3½″ x 57½″ (cut 2 on lengthwise grain)
	3½″ x 77½″ (cut 2 on lengthwise grain)
Turquoise print	Template Z: 40

Applique borders

Light blue solid	10″ x 86″ (cut 2)
	10″ x 106″ (cut 2)
Green print	bias strips (vines) 1½″ x 80″ (make 2)
	bias strips (vines) 1½″ x 105″ (make 2)
	bias strips (stems) 1″ x 15″ (make 24)
	Template AA: 100

Continued on next page

Continued

Light pink print	Template BB: 14
	Template DD: 20
Very dark pink	Template CC: 14
	Template DD: 10
Binding	10 crossgrain cuts 4″ wide

Cross & Crown

Pinwheel Square

Flying Darts

Godey Design

King David's Crown

All Kinds

Providence

Square & A Half

Album

Triangle Puzzle

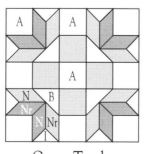

Goose Tracks

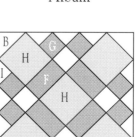

Domino Square

Acknowledgements

Thanks to the sisters in our pictures:

Victorian Silks ....Mabel and Irene Wells
(Photo courtesy of the Daughters of the Utah Pioneers Museum)
Buttons and Bows ....Susan and Shari Jo Stewart
Bright Colors ....Staci and Shari Watkins
Roses For Sue ....Karen and Leslie Neilson
Teddy Bears on Parade ....Robin, Megan, and Catlin Openshaw
Pinwheels and Posies ....Karen, Kristy, and Leslie Neilson
Sweet Sixteen ....Linda and Lisa Atwood
Duet ....Danielle and Erica Oldham
Friendship Basket ....Jennifer and Michelle West
Bridal Bouquet ....Joyce Stewart and Ann Winterton
Home Is Where You Hang Your Heart ....Caroline Winterton and Billie Jeanne Walmer
Nighttime Magic ....Kathryn Linder and Ramona Leishman
Fancy Free ....Elline Craig and Jeanne Huber
Calico Charm ....Ava Winterton and Nell Pearce
Memories ....Nina Ricks and Bertha Fullmer

Photographers: Joyce Stewart, Ann Seely, Alene Neilson, Wayne Winterton, John Atwood

References

Beyer, Jinny. *Patchwork Patterns*. EPM Publications, Inc., 1979.

Beyer, Jinny. *The Quilter's Album of Blocks and Borders*. EPM Publications, Inc., 1980.

Beyer, Jinny. *The Scrap Look*. EPM Publications, Inc., 1985.

Cory, Pepper. *Quilting Designs From the Amish*, C & T Publishing, P.O. Box 1456, Lafayette, CA 94549, 1985.

Hopkins, Judy and Nancy J. Martin. *Rotary Riot*. That Patchwork Place, 1991.

Hopkins, Mary Ellen. *It's OK If You Sit On My Quilt*. Yours Truly, 1982.

Horton, Roberta. *An Amish Adventure*. C & T Publishing, 1983.

Kimball, Jeana. *Applique Borders: An Added Grace*. That Patchwork Place, 1991.

Kimball, Jeana. *Reflections of Baltimore*. That Patchwork Place, 1991.

Mathieson, Judy. *Mariner's Compass*. C & T Publishing, 1987.

Quilter's Newsletter Magazine. February 1984.

Squire, Helen. *Dear Helen, Can You Tell Me?..all about quilting designs* American Quilter's Society, 1987.